Badminton
An Illustrated History

Jean-Yves GUILLAIN

Badminton
An Illustrated History

Translated by
Philippe Herridge, Heather Nielsen & Jean-Yves Guillain

Publibook

Dialoguez avec l'auteur, et retrouvez cet ouvrage accompagné de la critique de notre club de lecture, des commentaires des lecteurs, sur le site Publibook :

http://www.publibook.com

Publibook, Paris, 2004

Éditions Publibook,
14, rue des Volontaires
75015 Paris – France
Tél : 33 (0)1 53 69 65 55

IDDN.FR.010.0102955.000.R.P.2004.035.40000

Acknowledgements

The obstacles have been numerous in writing this book : rare and sparse sources, barely explored areas, frequent mistakes, and lack of interest in the history of sport… these are the reasons which could explain one getting lost in the maze of writing a book on the history of sport.

That is why advice and documents that come into one's path are particularly appreciated. My warmest thanks therefore go to Jill Brill, in charge of archives at the Badminton Association of England, to Rex Haggett, specialist of the shuttlecock game history, to Gerald Gurney, well-known collector and historian of racket sports, to Heather Nielsen for her deep knowledge of the iconography of this sport, to Olivier Magnani for his educational insights into Japanese society, and finally, to Christian Crémet for his encouragement and knowledge of French Badminton.

All have brought their bricks to the construction of this building, of which I have been the architect, and whose construction would have transformed itself into a Herculean task without their help.

Kick-Off

Like all the other sports, Badminton was not invented overnight.

In fact, it is not possible to trace the birth of a game or its transformation into a sport to a specific historical or geographical context with any precision.

A game's invention, *mutatis mutandis,* happens over time, undergoing continual modification according to particular circumstances. However, it is just as erroneous to believe in a single and eternal game, historically untraceable, which Adam and Eve would have played to pass the time.

Hitting a ball – or a shuttlecock for that matter – sending it to a particular place or over an obstacle, preventing your opponent from returning it or on the contrary, trying to keep the ball in play, these are essential elements of a recreational activity. Ball games play an important part in all cultures. Only special geographical or climatic conditions, or even ornithological (for shuttlecocks with feathers for example), have been able to hinder their development. These particular conditions apart, games have been omnipresent, even if they differ in form or contain special characteristics here and there.

The circumstances linked to game's evolution form such an entangled mess that it is futile to try to unravel them completely. However, this complexity cannot be ignored. It is important to attempt to reconstruct, demystify and analyse it in order to trace the origins of a sport, understand the changes in its evolution and explain its contemporary physical and cultural characteristics.

Badminton is no exception, on the contrary. The idea that it sprung to life suddenly in the last quarter of the nineteenth century and that like most other modern sports the British invented it is oversimplified.

In fact it is both true and false. It is true insofar as the game of Badminton as we know it today is very similar to the game played with a net, invented and developed by a handful of British officers at the turn of the century. It is false however if one considers its social and historical context, and the technical similarities which link it unmistakably to the "battledore and shuttlecock" game, an English and French recreational activity about which there are many references as far back as the fifteenth century. We must not overlook the games played with shuttlecock on other continents with the hand, the foot or a bat, and which also played an important role in defining the modern sport.

Badminton's development is therefore not linear. It is especially clouded by mysterious aspects that can partially explain its relative anonymity or at least the modest amount of media attention it generates in some parts of the world.

With such a rich and varied background history, spanning from France to Japan or from China to North America, Badminton could be one of the most ancient and universal of sports.

For this reason it was necessary to have a complete overview of its history focusing on its various stages of development rather than concentrating on technical or regulatory aspects. The important figures who have made up the world of Badminton ; its leaders and pioneers as well as the famous players who have graced its courts will, of course, be receiving the credit they deserve in this story.

Finally, the story will be dealing with the international recognition symbolised by its status as an Olympic sport, which for many has confirmed the universal dimension of Badminton.

The Match

Chapter 1 :
Universal and Distant origins

The first traces of a game involving the use of a shuttlecock can be found in Asia, and specifically in China.

Truths and myths surrounding the Chinese shuttlecock game

It supposedly has its origins in *T'su-chü,* a Football game created 2,500 years B.C at the time of the legendary Huang-Di (called The Yellow Emperor) in order to improve the skills of soldiers fighting Chi-You, the leader of the Miao people. According to the legend, Huang-Di laid down the foundations of Chinese civilisation, from the writing to Taoism, as well as the first medical treatise. This game, played with a round leather object filled with hair and mane, would achieve overnight popularity, inspiring poetic songs about heroes admired as gods.

With rules similar to Football the game with the shuttlecock called *Ti-jian-zi* consists of returning a shuttlecock with the foot. The kick can be executed either with the toe or the heel, with the foot or the knee.

This game exists on two levels : the players can return the shuttlecock from a stationary position and with one foot only. These players are called "little warriors". On a higher level, the "big warriors" favour kicking the shuttlecock while jumping off the ground.

This practice is very popular at the time of the Han and Tang dynasties (from 206 B.C to 907 A.D). Gradually, the game abandons its military context to become a winter sport performed by children in order to keep their bodies warm. In the 13th century, after the Sung dynasty, the game would adopt the name of *Chien-tsu* deriving from a Chinese expression meaning "arrow", which sounds the same as the word "shuttlecock".

The game develops over the following centuries to such an extent that it became one of the most sought-after physical activities in the Chinese Empire, regardless of sex and social class.

Its fame would spread as far as Europe as the article "The game of the shuttlecock in China" published by F. Dillaye in *Le Journal de la Jeunesse* testifies in 1875. He disapproves of this game due to an insufficiently feminine character : "*I confess that it seems to be easier to play the Japanese shuttlecock game than its Chinese equivalent, although in the Celestial Empire this game is preferred by women and children. Don't these strange players think of throwing the shuttlecock with the sole of their laced-boot ? Oh dear, maidens of China, this is so unsuitable ! No matter how much you tell me that your shuttlecock made out of a piece of leather rolled into a ball, threaded with metal strands to make it heavier and ornamented with three long feathers inserted into pierced holes cannot be played with a racket, I don't accept your excuses. Take after our young French maidens ; remain graceful at all times*".

Over the centuries the shuttlecock has been made of various materials. The feathers come from chickens but the base is made out of pieces of wool, leather or snake skin. It is weighted down with little pieces of metal or coins.

The spreading
of the "shuttlecock-kicking" game to other Asian territories

From China the "shuttlecock-kicking" game migrates to other Asian countries.

In Taiwan, shuttlecock-kicking evolves particularly at the time of the Han dynasty (206 B.C to 220 A.D) and is today one of the most popular of traditional sports. In Korea, the game is called *Jeigi-chagi*. At the end of the 19th century, Stewart Culin, the traditional game specialist states that the shuttlecock is made from a cotton ball flattened and filled with ashes or clay with a pheasant's feather stuck in the top. In winter, the game is a favourite pastime of shopkeepers who appreciate this efficient way of keeping their feet warm.

In Vietnam wood carvings of shuttlecock players were found in temples dating back to the 17th century. A century earlier a poet would praise the town of Hanoi by describing its attractive features and its continuous animation :

"The sound of flutes springing from the palace makes the moonlight tremble,
The drums in watch towers urge the flowers to open.
The markets are more and more animated,
The streets rival one another in beauty,
Young men tuck up their tunics and play shirtless shuttlecock...."

("Spring in the royal city", 1508, Nguyen Gian Thanh).

We come across the shuttlecock game also in Macao where it is called *Chiquia* and in Malaysia under the name of *Chap-teh* where the feathers are replaced by the marzipan or hibiscus flower.

The game is also played in Thailand. The English governess at the Royal Court, Anna Harriette Leonowens indeed described it as one of the most popular sports along with boxing, horse-racing and croquet (*The English Governess at the Siamese Court being Recollections of Six Years in the Royal Palace at Bangkok*, 1870).

In fact variations of the shuttlecock game exist in Asia. The Miao people, between China and Thailand, prefer to use a wooden bat carved in a primitive fashion to play with a shuttlecock made of bamboo (called *nbi*) into which are inserted three feathers.

It is at this point that the game starts to resemble the shuttlecock game with wooden racket adopted by the Japanese for many centuries.

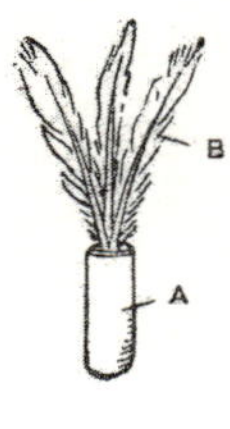

In Japan : from game to ritual

Japan has been a keen participant of the shuttlecock game for a long time. But unlike the Celestial Empire, as if to distinguish itself better, the country of the Rising Sun plays it with a wooden bat called *hagoita.*

The crown Prince Sadafusa's newspaper mentions a shuttlecock event played at the court in 1432 between two teams, one feminine the other masculine. The game undergoes further transformation during the Muromachi period (1338 – 1573), when the racket adopts a trapezoidal shape. During this time, to commemorate the New Year, there is a match at the Royal Palace called *Kokinoko shôbu.*

The bats are ornamented with traditional drawings. They originally represent sabres, jewels or gods. Colours and delicate patterns with gold or silver lining would be added around the time of Genroku (1688 – 1704, Edo period). They depict scenes representing the *sagichô,* a New Year ritual taking place the 15th and 18th of January at the Imperial Palace. Some eyewitness accounts relate that the bats (*sagichô hagoita)* are sometimes thrown into the fire with other offerings. Another author, Saikaku, recounts that in 1692 "shuttlecock boards" made in Kyoto are sold at the great end of year market. As the bats become more and more ornamented their recreational use declined ; from being leisure instruments they would become essentially ornaments for young girls to celebrate the New Year.

In order to play this game *(Hanetsuki),* the Japanese use a shuttlecock comprising a small rounded coin and feathers. The shape of the shuttlecock, resembling the head of a dragonfly when hit, is explained by its use as a device to protect children from mosquito bites. The game can also have as its source the ritual of throwing soya beans on the last day of winter - the original name of the bat being "racket for barbaric demons" and used to chase away evil spirits. Later, it is used to throw the seed of the soap-berry tree into which several small feathers are fastened (hence their name *hane*).

The shuttlecocks are also referred to as "small barbaric demons". Indeed, in his book *Segen mondô* published in 1544, Ichijô Furuya refers to the shuttlecock game as "the game of the little barbaric demons". The shuttlecock was also be made out of pieces of bamboo cut into strings the width of a hair or even small trunks of bamboo filled with paper.

Officially, this game can be played in two ways ; the *Oibane* game (literally "shuttlecock-chasing") involves the use of a minimum of two players taking it in turns to send each other the shuttlecock ; the *Tsukibane* game (or "shuttlecock-hitting") for one player only, consists of bouncing the shuttlecock off his racket as many times as possible.

Traces of the shuttlecock game in North America

The shuttlecock game is not confined to Asia only. It has long been played in various parts of America, although in a variety of forms.

It is one of the favourite games of several of the North-American Indian tribes. The Zuñi (from the region of New Mexico) play with shuttlecocks made of corn husks and pierced with feathers. Indeed, one of these feathers has been found in a cave dwelling house in the Chelly Canyon.

The *Po-ke-an* uses green corn husks neatly interlaced and wrapped into a flat square about an inch to two inches square, and on one side is placed two upright feathers. The shuttlecock is hit with the palm of the hand. It must stay as long as possible in the air while the players encourage each other by counting aloud in their native language : *"to-pa, quil-e, hi, a-we-ta, ap-ti... "*. A variation of this game, the *Po-ki-nanane*, is so-called because of the noise produced by the contact between hand and shuttlecock is similar to the noise of the tread of a jack rabbit upon frozen snow. The rules are very basic. The participants must hit a pre-determined number of strikes : *"One bets that he can toss the shuttlecock a given number of times. While ten is the number specially associated with the game, the wagers are often made for twenty, fifty, and sometimes a hundred throws. In case of failure the other player tries his skill, each party alternating in the game until one or the other tosses the shuttlecock (only one hand being used) the given number of times, which entitles him to the game"*.

The Piman Natives of Arizona also play the game with the hand under the name of *Kwaitusiwikut.* Pre-historical traces of the game have even been found in the region of Four Corners, at the border between Utah, Colorado, New Mexico, and Arizona where the Anasazi tribe settled. Ancestors of modern Pueblo people, this civilisation flourished from 200 to 1300 A.D. Although their main occupation was to cultivate corn, in their free time the Anasazis held running races and hit shuttlecock (with the hand). These recreational activities were held at village feasts and religious celebrations involving several villages.

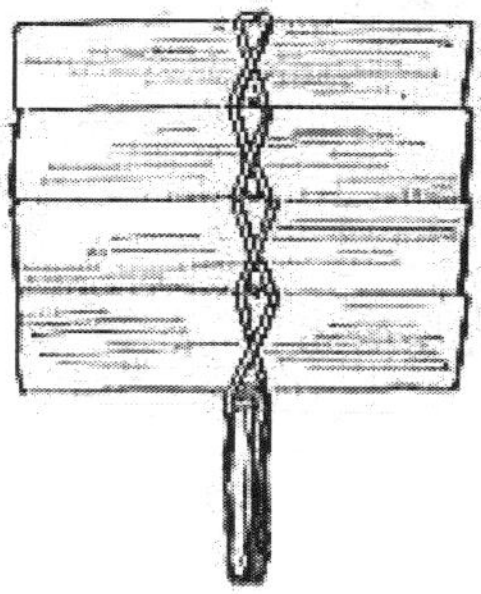

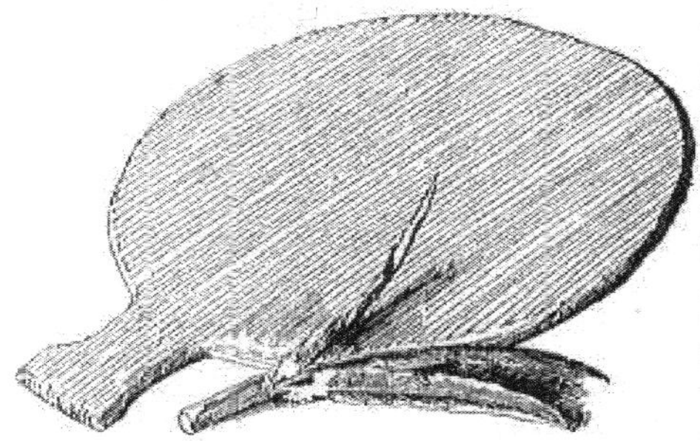

In British Columbia and around Washington, the Bellacoola, Hesquiaht, Nimkish, and Kwakiutl tribes use a special kind of racket. Stewart Culin's observations in the 24th Annual Report of the Bureau of Ethnology in 1903 are full of descriptions of the different kinds of bats and shuttlecocks used by the West Coast Indians.

As for the rackets, they are either made out of pieces of wood attached together and fixed to the handle, or a plank of wood carved into the shape of a bat. The shuttlecock comprises of three feathers inserted into a wooden branch stem. To play the *Kwakiutl* tribe's version of the game (*Quumla*), two or more players have to stand in a circle. The shuttlecock is thrown in front and to the right of the players and the winner is the one who could keep the shuttlecock in the air the longest. In typical tribal fashion these matches are played by the boys as well the girls.

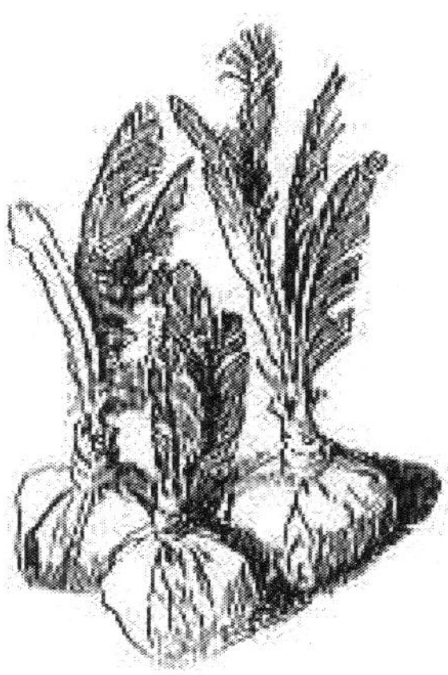

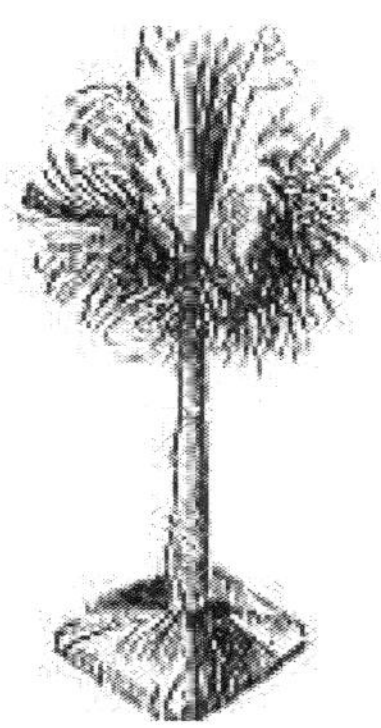

In The Fraser Valley, the Sto : lo have a traditional game providing the opportunity for people to compete in a physical activity while reinforcing their knowledge about the natural world. Two people play the *Ts'eqwela*, each holding a 25-cm long paddle carved out of cedar. The shuttlecock can be a small round rock with cedar boughs tied around it or a piece of light elder-wood trimmed with three feathers on its end.

The aim is still to keep the shuttlecock in the air longer than the opponent. However the objective is not confined to entertainment. While hitting the shuttlecock each player has to name a part of a fish. The game is won or lost either when the shuttlecock falls to the ground or when a fish part is repeated or cannot be named.

Northern Peru and its ceremonial variant

The game also exists for centuries in the South American continent.

Before the conquest of North Peru by the Incas, other civilisations developed. One of these called Mochica and flourishing between 200 and 700 A.D, has left traces of an original version of the shuttlecock game. Illustrated vase drawings indicate a ritual game employing a shuttlecock of feathers attached to a small round wooden disc by a cord. This cord is wrapped around a long wooden rod and used to throw the round-feathered object into the air : *"This is a festive game in which a shuttlecock attached to a staff is cast aloft with a throwing stick to float through the air like a balloon".*

In fact this is more of a fertility ritual than a sport event, but according to the ethnologists, the use of a feathered "shuttlecock" provides an unmistakable link to the game of Badminton : *"Races and Badminton games were important ceremonies which were inaugurated by the gods and now in accordance with this commission were executed by men. There are reasons to suspect that the strange Badminton game of the ancient culture of Moche may have been connected with the ideas concerning the growth of the fruits of the field".*

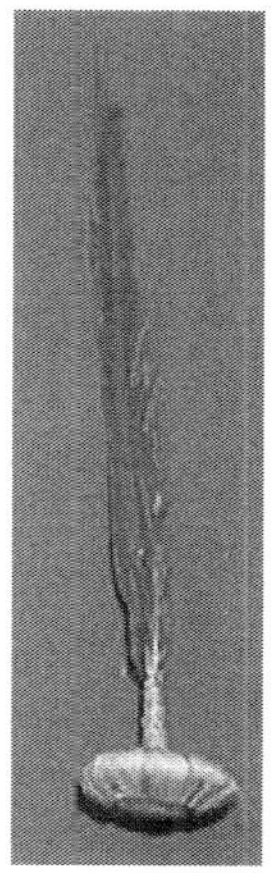

The Amazonian game of hand shuttlecock

The feathered ball game spreads to other parts of Latin America, especially in Amazonia (Guyana), eastern Brazil and in the Gran Chaco (divided among Paraguay, Bolivia, and Argentina). The Tupis play *Peteca* with stones wrapped in leaves inside an ear of corn or a leather pad with feathers. For the Bororo Indians the shuttlecock game is a collective leisure activity played in public – all village members can participate in the game that takes place in the yard.

No lesser observer than Theodore Roosevelt witnesses the game at the beginning of the 20th century. During his trip across western Brazil in 1914, he relates the following scene during an important religious ceremony : "*The children play about with unconcern throughout the ceremony, one throwing high in the air and again, then catching in his hands a loaded feather, a kind of shuttlecock".*

Meso-America : the alternative of the rubber ball

In Latin America, however, the shuttlecock game doesn't have the same success as the other types of games played with a ball hit with the hand or a bat. The Incas play ball games, like the Aztecs who invent throughout North America various types of games involving a rubber ball.

Nevertheless the Aztecs, taking inspiration from the Mexican wildlife, are at the origin of the feather civilisation. Working the feather has religious overtones (see the famous god Quetzalcoat, "snake of quetzal feathers" or even Huitzilopochtli, "fly-bird"), and produces magnificent ceremonial robes. This would have favoured the development of a shuttlecock game.

Traces would indeed be left in their *codexes*, these being famous painted manuscripts from Meso-America, in skin or fibres, about literature, astronomy, or history. The shuttlecock thus appears several times in the codex Borbonicus. This object of five quetzal's emerald green feathers, the emblematic bird from the Aztec civilisation, looks very much like a shuttlecock.

However, it seems to be more a decoration illustrating wealth or the birth of a baby boy. Indeed, unlike the rubber ball game (*Ulama),* very popular before the Spanish conquest, there are neither images showing players in action, nor precise descriptions of the game by the first visitors to the region at the beginning of the 16th century, nor existing archaeological material (bats or clay sculptures of players).

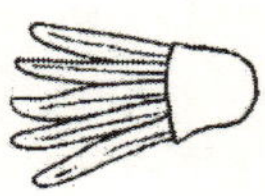

The shuttlecock game is therefore universal. It is particularly rooted in the popular Asian and American traditions and customs. However, its rules are not the same everywhere. The shuttlecock travels from one player to the next under the impulse of the foot, the hand or the bat. The rule is nevertheless the same ; sending each other the shuttlecock without it touching the floor. Its importance is not only geographical. For certain civilisations the ritual and ceremonial aspects of the game are of more importance than the game's graceful qualities.

Nevertheless, the recreational aspect is of supreme importance to the shuttlecock game as it would be played in Europe after the middle ages.

Chapter 2 :
Social and Recreational Recognition of "Battledore & Shuttlecock"

As far as ball games go, the Middle Ages doesn't innovate, but improves or gives structure to ancient Greek or Roman games (*Phaeninde, Harpaste*).

We know that ball games are played in ecclesiastical French society, even if they are rarely mentioned between the 11th and 13th centuries. These leisure activities are defined by the part of the body used to play it, in other words the bare hand (hence "*Jeu de paume*").

The first mention of a game with ball struck with the hand appears in the second half of the 13th century. There are enough people playing this game to justify special handy craft manufacture of these balls called *esteufs*. At the beginning the main players comprise the aristocracy before spreading the popularity spreads increasingly.

From the palm game to the racket game

As the ball is hard and heavy (in order to bounce better and last longer), it becomes necessary to protect the palm of the hand from injury. This leads to the invention of a glove, occasionally double-lined for greater protection and fixed to the hand by a piece of leather.

The use of bats or rackets gradually appears in order to further facilitate the striking of the ball and increase the speed. A first clear mention of the racket dates from 1505, in a text evoking a game between the Castillan King Philippe le Beau and the Lord Marquis of Dorset.

Two types of rackets coexist at this time : on the one hand simple wooden bats covered with vellum ; on the other hand rackets with handles and wooden frames equipped with strings. The status of 16th century ball and rackets makers clearly illustrates these points. These rackets are master-pieces of craftsmanship, which are made according to the strict regulations, giving full recognition in this field. Another uncommon group fabricates balls, rackets and shuttlecocks independently of the games room ; the brushmaker who also sells rackets and feathers in order to beat fabrics and carpets.

The game, initially played outdoors, becomes increasingly adapted to specially built indoor halls. Most of the English and French palaces would soon be equipped with such games rooms.

The *Jeu de paume* would pave the way for other types of games : Lawn Tennis, *Pelote basque*, Fives, Squash, *Balle au tamis* and of course Badminton.

In fact, the battledore & shuttlecock game and the *Jeu de paume* have parallel histories. Firstly because they both involve the use of a bat or a racket. Also, because the rackets, balls and shuttlecocks are made by the same craftsmen and according to the same high demands of manufacture, at least when destined for use by the upper classes. Finally, because the participants can take pleasure from playing both games.

The first accounts of the shuttlecock game played on a regular basis

During the Renaissance, François 1st, King of France from 1515 to 1547, plays both games equally well. The shuttlecock game is known as *Coquantin*, a term originating from the two long cock feathers generally used to decorate the shuttlecock. However, in the Kingdom of France the shuttlecock has other names.

As the shuttlecock rotates when travelling from one racket to the other, it is called *Pilvotiau* by the Champenois. In other regions such as Anjou, the shuttlecock is called *Grièche* as it is decorated with feathers of this bird or because the arrangement of the feathers reminds one of it. In the region of Lyon, the shuttlecock is called *Picandeau* because it is decorated with magpie feathers, alternating black and white.

In 1534, François Rabelais publishes a list of all the games played by the young Gargantua in *La vie très horrifique du grand Gargantua, père de Pantagruel.* The *Cocquantin* and the *Picandeau* are mentioned. The first reference to racket strings, the use of which is starting to split the game in two, is also to be found in Rabelais : *"On croyt le premier qui dict si l'esteuf est sus ou soubz la corde" ("he's believed who first said the ball is out or under the line"*). As for the net as it is known today in Tennis, it appears around 1600.

In 1552, there is a drawing made of Charles Maximilien (the future Charles IX) at the age of two, holding a racket. Bearing in mind his young age, we can assume that it is the racket of the shuttlecock game and not the *Jeu de paume*.

The shuttlecock game has similar success in England where it is called "battledore & shuttlecock" or "drum-bat" if the racket is wooden covered with vellum of goat or cow skin.

The works of Joseph Strutt recount the existence of a miniature drawing from the 14th century in which two young peasants hit the shuttlecock to each other with rackets. The game, mainly played outdoors at this time and in an unlimited area, would be very popular with 16th century children. A recreational activity more than a competition, the aim is to make the rallies last as long as possible.

The game achieves such popularity that in Leicester the "Shrove Tuesday" becomes known as "shuttlecock day". The young boys and girls joyfully hit shuttlecocks all day long. In the villages of the West Riding in Yorkshire the streets are filled with grow-up men and women on the second Sunday of May to play battledore & "shuttlefeathers". At Wakefield, Yorkshire, the children chant with each hit, the sentences being repeated until the shuttlecock falls :

"1st. This year, next year, long time, never
2nd. Monday, Tuesday, Wednesday, Thursday, Friday, Saturday, Sunday
3rd. Tinker, tailor, soldier, sailor, rich man, poor man, beggar-man, thief
4th. Silk, satin, cotton, rags
5th. Cocch, carriage, wheelbarrow, donkey-cart"

In Deptford, the rhymes were as follows :
"Grandmother, grandmother, tell me no lie, how many children before I die ? One, two, three" or even *"Tell me the truth, how many years have I been to school ? One, two three"*

In London, the rhythms are :
"One, two, buckle my shoe,
Three, four, knock at the door,
Five, six, pick up sticks,
Seven, eight, lay them straight,
Nine, ten, a good fat hen,
Eleven, twelve, ring the bell,
Thirteen, fourteen, maids a courting,
Fifteen, sixteen, maids in the kitchen,
Seventeen, eighteen, mistress waiting,
Nineteen, twenty, my plate's empty"

In the English countryside as well as in London, the battledore and shuttlecock game fills both a recreational and a prophetic role for the young children keen to know what the future held in store.

The game's social status rises during the 17th century, as it becomes royalty's favourite pastime. This fact is revealed in 1609 in the play *The History of Two Maids of Moreclacke*. The author and Shakespearean actor, Robert Armin, has one of the character's say : "*to play shuttlecock methinks is the game now*".

Illustrating battledore's importance as a recreational activity for the English aristocracy, a story relates that Prince Henry, the son of King James 1st (1566-1625, King of England in 1603), accidentally hits his opponent *"playing at shittle-cock with one farr taller than himself"*.

Another observer during the reign of James 1st, describing the relative prestige of the different games of this time, states that "*in the early 17th century, King James 1st, forbade anybody in his court to play these violent games. Other popular games are battledore, shuttlecock, leapfrog, seesaw, bowling the hoop... as well as swimming and fishing. Tennis and billiards are played in noble households*".

The spreading of battledore and shuttlecock among the European aristocracy

The shuttlecock is also fashionable in other European kingdoms. Queen Kristina of Sweden (1626-1689) loves this game passionately and imposes it on the most important people at her court. She manages to convince the French protestant theologian and geographer Samuel Bochart to play during his stay in Stockholm in 1652. Kristina forces the members of the court to abandon their frocks and wigs *"and the shuttlecock is passed from one racket to the next, fluttering in the air to the Queen's immense satisfaction"*.

The game is spreading throughout the French court too. The Marquees of Sévigné (1626-1696) declares in her diary *"I played shuttlecock and thousands of other little games"*. The Duchess of Montpensier, a distant cousin of Louis XIV, tells in her 1653 memoirs : "*His Majesty went to Blois and I to Saint-Fargeau. I was there in a day. The ladies and I wore feathered bonnets ; I had seen this invention for the first time hunting with Madame de Sully. We had lengthened or shortened it to render it beautiful. M. de Bellegarde, who lives just a few miles from Saint-Fargeau, would often come. After the play, the shuttlecock game got underway. As I like physical exercise I played two hours in the morning and two hours after dinner. Madame de Frontenac and I played incessantly though she always finished by beating me although I improved my game as we went along"*.

The Marquis of Dangeau who is close to King Louis XIV, makes several references to the King's liking for the shuttlecock game in his 1684-1686 chronicles : "*The King spent the day beating opponents at games of shuttlecock and culbas ; M. de Bourbon and M. de Vendôme had the honour of accompanying him*". A little later : "*Monseigneur went to sleep at Valery, at M. le Duc de Bourbon's ; on arrival he beat opponents, and in the evening he played shuttlecock and culbas*". Philippe de Champaigne of the Flemish school even paints a portrait of a young Louis XIV holding a racket and a shuttlecock.

Adored by the nobility, but increasingly by the working classes too, the game quickly becomes a literary subject. A romantic poem by Guillaume Colletet dated 1656 and simply entitled *Le Jeu de Volant* perfectly illustrates this :

"One day that my beloved Cloris with newly-acquired grace,
A racket in her hand pushed me to shuttlecock,
Suspended in flight and twisting and turning,
Instead of coming to me stayed by her.

What are you doing my immortal nymph ? I asked,
How is it that your arm is so weak and slow,
That mine sends it to you (...)
If my hand flashes are full of uncertainty
That my eye flashes reach the heart"

The educational value of the game of battledore and shuttlecock

At the beginning of the 18th century, besides its value as a recreational pastime or social event, it also begins to be recognised for its physical and educational virtues.

The great 18th century thinker Fenelon, realising the game's potential as entertainment for children, emphasises the necessity for granting more importance to the feather game : "*The activities which have the most success are those involving body movement ; boys and girls are happy as long as they change places often : a shuttlecock or a ball is enough*". He adds, however, that it is important to discourage games "*exciting the passions*" and involving intense competition.

Rousseau on the contrary holds a different position. He warmly recommends natural exercise provided by old-style games : Mail, *Paume*, bow and arrow, ball games, but is critical of battledore as follows : "*when a child plays shuttlecock he practices hand and eye co-ordination ; but he learns nothing. You prefer the shuttlecock because it is harmless and less tiring ? You are mistaken. The shuttlecock is a woman's game ; but there isn't one who hits a moving ball. The white skins mustn't be roughened by violence ; but we, who are vigorous and robust, cannot be so without sweat and how do we expect to defend ourselves if we are never attacked ?*"

Rousseau thus demonstrates that the *Jeu de paume* (called "Real" or "Royal Tennis") is excellent for men : "*we play lazily when there is no danger. A falling shuttlecock doesn't harm anyone. But nothing awakes the arm so much as having to cover the head ; nothing livens reactivity so much as having to protect the eyes. Throwing oneself from one side of the room to the other, predicting a ball's bounce when still in the air, returning it with a sure and firm hand ; such games educate men more than anything else*" (*Emile*).

In the 18th century battledore and shuttlecock, after having been for so long a game without exact rules, played both in dark alleys and in regal palaces, begins to adopt a precise form and regulation. The similarities with the *Jeu de paume* which already exist through racket and ball manufacture, are strengthened further from the moment the game is played in indoor real Tennis courts.

In his 1767 book *The Art of Tennis Racket Maker*, Garsault only mentions the art of the shuttlecock "*because it is played in a Tennis court, instead of Real Tennis*". We also learn that "*the game had been particularly fashionable at the time of the Duke of Orleans, Regent of the Realm ; it was his favourite game*".

Eight people can play indoors, but the game is best with four or six. The rules are as follows : "*Large shuttlecocks, two inches in diameter at the base, and with feathers $2^{1/2}$ inches long are used. One serves with the racket as in the Jeu de paume. From the sidewall of the service-side is stretched a second cord and net, three feet from the real one and parallel with it. An attendant of the court serves ; for this he stands at the door of the hazard-side. The service is given in two ways ; the attendant either throws the shuttlecock into the air with his hands to the server, or else he uses the crank. It is forbidden to send the shuttlecock against the walls or throw it between the two cords.*"

This information is of capital importance. At the beginning of the 18th century and more than one century before the invention of the modern game of Badminton, it seems that the game of battledore and shuttlecock has acquired the use of a net as an accessory.

At the time of the French Revolution, this game reaches its noble status. This would enable the Count Rivarol (1753 – 1801) to write : "*How I'd like to be a shuttlecock to be able to stroke generous uncovered breasts and come to rest at the foot of young beauties*".

The game of battledore and shuttlecock as a literary and artistic subject

There are more and more pictures and engravings depicting it. In the second half of the 18th century the French artists Gravelot, Duplessis-Bertaux, and Jean-Siméon Chardin as well as the Hungarian painter Adam Manyoki use the famous game as a subject for their paintings.

At the beginning of the 19th century, the game's popularity is very high. It is included in every good behaviour guide for children and adolescents.

X. le Prince, in his book *Jeux des Jeunes filles de tous les pays* (1823), devotes a chapter to battledore and shuttlecock, emphasising its qualities, as it constitutes a pleasant form of physical exercise both outside when the weather is fine and indoors when it is less favourable. "*This game is played in the open air when the weather is fine, as well as inside apartments. If a group of people feel like playing this game, all they need is a shuttlecock and two bats. They can also play a version with two shuttlecocks.*"

Never lacking in ideas, the fans of this game are soon trying out variations of this game. According to H.R. d'Allemagne (1889), some players *"use a stick to receive the shuttlecock on its pointed side. Three inches from the point there is a hook that stops the shuttlecock from sliding down the stick. In this version the shuttlecock has a special shape. It is a hard wooden ring on which feathers are implanted"*.

In *Moeurs de province* (1857) however Flaubert refers to the traditional shuttlecock game when he has Mrs Bovary say : "*During those beautiful summer nights when the warm streets are empty and servants are playing shuttlecock on doorsteps, he opened the window and leant against it. The river, making this neighbourhood into a little Venice, was flowing (...)*".

In one of Emile Zola's works (*La conquête de Plassans)* the young secular priest Surin and two young middle-class maidens play a few rallies : *"They went out and the most delightful game got underway. The two maidens began. Angeline was the first to miss the shuttlecock. Surin who replaced her held the racket with majestic expertise. He had brought his cloak between his legs ; he jumped forward, behind, on the side, scooped up the shuttlecock barely off the ground, struck it on the backhand at an impressive height, thrust it forward straight or made it cut elegant curves, calculated with perfect science."*

Proof of its success, the game is frequently used as a metaphor in literary works. Two such examples can be found in Balzac and Hugo : "*A political event, a trial, street songs, an actor's play, all is destined to maintain this spirit which consists of taking words and ideas as shuttlecocks and sending them around on rackets" (Le Père Goriot*, Balzac). "*I wasn't made to be a Parisian, forever bouncing like a shuttlecock between two rackets from the lazy group to the noisy one"* (*Les Misérables*, Hugo).

The game itself enters a new era in the 19th century. From an educational and pleasant pastime it would become an organised athletic sport. The old game of battledore and shuttlecock becomes Badminton.

MAY THE
NEW YEAR
BRING YOU JOY

Chapter 3 :
Birth of the Anglo-Indian Game of Badminton

Modern Badminton seems to have originated in India and been created there by the British during the colonial period towards the end of the 19th century.

The first Badminton matches in India

A photo taken in India in 1867 enables us to trace its birth to the second half of the 1860's. This photo shows several Englishmen playing shuttlecock in the open-air. A net, an accessory that allows us to distinguish between the new game of Badminton and the traditional game of battledore and shuttlecock, separates them

According to certain sources, Badminton is played in various parts of India : Madras, Bombay, Peshawar and Calcutta. The game is known as *Tomfool* (derived from a local game *tam tam,* and *phul* which means "flower" in allusion to the shuttlecock) or as *Poonai,* because it is played a lot in Poona, at that time an important British military base.

Two variations are catalogued at this time. The first is played with balls of wool. This game is played in the 1850's by the upper classes, and notably by the Prince of Tanjore's family thus contributing to its popularity. The game is known locally as *Pooppanthu vilyattam,* probably due to the flowery appearance of the yellow woollen balls.

The balls are made in such a way that they can reach the edges of the court when hit effortlessly. They are made by Indian women from two pieces of cardboard cut around the edge of a sherry glass and covered with several layers of wool to the desired size. These balls are preferred to the shuttlecock in windy or wet conditions. The English would baptise this new game "Ball Badminton".

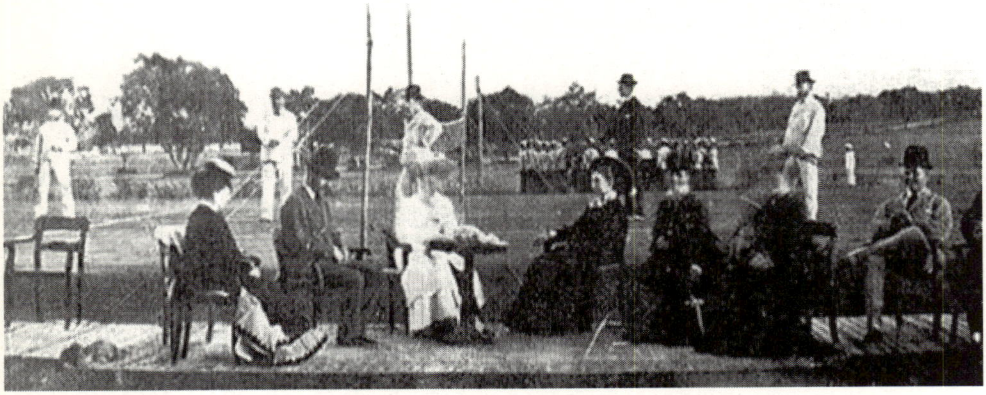

The English influence in India is very strong at this time, particularly in military circles, and this is responsible for the Indian game borrowing the shuttlecock from the traditional "battledore & shuttlecock" game which is played a lot in 19th century England.

Modern Badminton seems therefore to derive from two sources : firstly, the net, lines, and rules of "Ball Badminton" ; secondly, the shuttlecock and different types of bats (wood, skin and string) from "battledore and shuttlecock".

Invention of commonly-used rules

The game of Badminton begins to make a name for itself with the use of the shuttlecock in 1873. On May 31st, a reader runs an advertisement in the magazine *The Field* in order to know more about *"the Badminton game of battledore"* fashionable in India and which he has recently heard about.

A lot of replies are published in the subsequent issues of *The Field*, all coming from British expatriates residing in or having spent some time in India. They describe a game with a basic common identity but with variations depending on where it is played.

One account tells of a game played by four players in a room separated by a piece of string about four feet or more high from the floor. The winner is the first to reach 15 points. The aim is to prevent the opponent from returning the shuttlecock and of course the shuttlecock must always be hit over the string. The suggestion is then made to hang some sheets of paper from the string, or else to use a net, in order to ensure that the shuttlecock flies over and not under the string, thereby avoiding disputes between the two sides.

In October 1873, a certain Major Forbes sends to *The Field* a short pamphlet entitled *A Handbook of Badminton* with rules for playing the game. The book is published at Calcutta by the Great Eastern Hotel Company. His version of the game is in fact a mixture of several local rules in use at the time, and presented in such a way to facilitate the playing of the game by ladies. *"The rules embodied in this handbook have been framed from a careful study of those generally in force at present in different places, and which upon the whole, have been found to answer best and to give the most general satisfaction (...) I am aware that the size of the courts and of the ground laid down in this handbook is very different to that which is gener-*

ally in force. This arrangement was originally adopted with the view of making the game as fair as possible for ladies when playing against gentlemen".

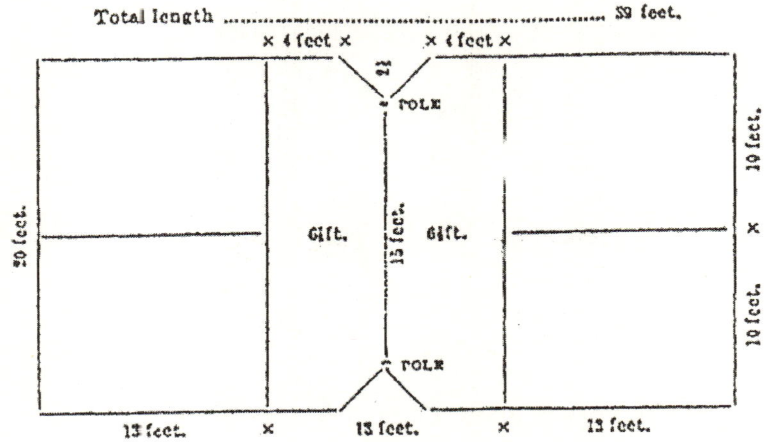

The number of players varies from two to six or more, but with even sides. The court is rectangular and drawn in chalk. A level piece of ground has to be selected, and a space of 28 feet long by 20 feet broad marked out on it by means of pegs and strings. The four courts, each 10 feet square, are then laid off in the same manner. The courts are separated by a piece of neutral ground, 20 feet by 8 feet, so that two courts are left close together on one side of it. The shuttlecock must not fall into this neutral zone. The first team to reach 15 points is the winner. If the score reaches 13 points each, the teams can opt to play a tiebreak with the first to five as the winner. The server is allowed three attempts at serving (rule 10), provided that in doing so he doesn't either hit or touch the shuttlecock with his bat.

Another reader later portrays a version of the game as played in Nagpore. The diagram shows another rectangular court. It is recommended to play two against two but the court can be made bigger to accommodate four against four. If the shuttlecock touches the net the game can continue. This correspondent stipulates that the game is especially designed to be played by women calling it "ladies' rackets" : *"this game has entirely superseded croquet in this part of the world".*

In Murree in the Punjab region, there are 21 rules codified. Its most distinguishing feature is the court, which is in the shape of an "hourglass". The upper margin of the net is 5 feet from the ground measured between the poles. The term "clean over the net" means that the shuttlecock must not touch anything, or any person, on its way from battledore to the other side of the net. The game is in three sets and up to 15 points.

Two types of court are therefore used in India : the rectangular court and the hourglass shape. The latter proves so popular that it would dominate the former for 30 years and would be used for the first official competitions in England. The rectangular version would only reach full recognition at the beginning of the 20th century. However, one of the few engravings of Badminton at this time and used to illustrate an article in *The Graphic* shows a rectangular court.

Although the games are mainly played outside on grass, the indoor game is also evolving. In 1909, J.H.E. Hart who participated in the game's development in Karachi, relates that some matches were played in abandoned army camps and that the hour-glass court had to be used due to having to keep camp doors open courtside.

The English gradually import the game with its Indian rules. Much advice is given about how to adapt the game to the English climate. An English solicitor writes in *The Field* that all-weather courts can easily be built in cement or cobblestone for less than 100 pounds.

Mystery and controversy about the origin of the name "Badminton"

Where does the name "Badminton" come from ? It comes from the Somerset family's Badminton House situated near the village of Badminton.

The Duke of Beaufort's Gloucestershire home "Badminton House" has for a long time been a popular location for the game. Hand-written scores on the vellum bats testify that the family children established records : 2.117 rallies in 1830, 2.018 in 1845. According to certain sources, the 7th Duke of Beaufort's children would make the rallies more difficult by putting a string across the middle of the hall. However, in the absence of evidence testifying to this innovation, it is more reasonable to assert that the children continued to hit the shuttlecock to each other implementing the old battledore and shuttlecock rules.

According to other writers, modern Badminton is born out of the initiative of army officers from India during a stay at Badminton House. One rainy day they decided to combine the Indian game's rules and its woollen balls, with the Beaufort's children's shuttlecock and bats.

A family friend, John Loraine Baldwin, a keen sportsman and writer of sports rules (the laws of short whist in 1864) is supposed to have standardised the new game during one of his visits to Badminton House, baptising this new leisure activity "Badminton".

If we base ourselves therefore on existing and tangible evidence, it seems fair to trace the game's source to army officers based in India while attributing its name to the Somerset's household.

The game's importation and development in England

It is certain that the game develops in England as officers serving in India take their retirement.

In 1875, a club is opened in Folkestone, Kent. One of the members is a certain Lieutenant Seymour S.C. Dolby (born 1851, Kent), the future founder of the Badminton Association. The club meets in the ballroom of the West Cliff Hotel where tea and Badminton are the favourite pastimes. In Devonshire, General Sir Alfred Lucas is the "pioneer". At first, the matches take place outside but the need for indoor courts and clubs with allocated spaces soon becomes apparent. Other clubs soon open in Teignmouth, Bath, Southsea and Guildford.

At the same time, attempts to standardise the game increase. In 1876, the first brochure is published. It is devoted both to Badminton and another game in the process of development, Tennis. Although edited under the name Cavendish, this collection of rules is in fact the work of the journalist Henry Jones. The section devoted to Badminton is five pages long and has the title "The Anglo-Indian Game of Badminton", illustrating the game's diverse origins. The number of players varies from four to eight. The hourglass court is used and the games are up to 15 points. And *"a net suspended between two upright poles takes the place of the horizontal bar, and the players stand as of yore in courts on either side (...) Any garden that has but*

a small lawn provides the suitable locus in quo, a few minutes suffice to erect the necessary apparatus, and then, given a fair sky and a happy, lighted-hearted company – Badminton will furnish healthy enjoyable recreation and amusement for both old and young of both sexes for many a summer's afternoon".

In 1876, J. Buchanan's book *Lawn-Tennis and Badminton* is published. Buchanan, a maker of sport and leisure equipment, outlines two great advantages Badminton has over cricket : fewer players and possible female participation.

Two years later, in a book with the same title, Julian Marshall emphasises the characteristics the shuttlecock must have in order to improve its use outdoors. He also advocates adopting the points system used for Tennis.

In the same year, 1878, H. Day, racket master at The Oval, Kennington, suggests other rules. Contrary to existing rules, the server is given three chances to serve correctly to the other side (rule 8). The matches are up to 15 or 21. Day gives demonstrations of the game at a fee of five guineas per night.

In 1883, in *Lawn Tennis, Croquet, Rackets etc.,* Badminton is above all described as an open air game preferably played on grass rather than asphalt. The rules are flexible and determined by the conditions or by the participants themselves : this includes decisions regarding the height of the net, the size of the court, or the number of the players. Contrary to existing practices the author depicts a rectangular court. During this period, Badminton is still having trouble distinguishing itself from the traditional game of battledore and shuttlecock. In fact the writer suggests that it is just as interesting to settle for returning the shuttlecock, as it is to try to hit it out of the opponent's reach.

In 1887, J.H.E. Hart adapts the "Indian rules" to the indoor facilities of the Bath Club. He would repeat this procedure in 1890 with the help of Mr Bagnel-Wild.

Badminton soon spreads from southern England to London and its region. The players use squash or Tennis rackets. Three to five players are allowed on each side. Famous players such as Stewart M. Massey or Albert D. Prebble will soon develop their skills in this club, and other clubs are established in Crystal Palace and Blackheath.

Despite the organisation of an inter-club match between Southsea and Bath in the 1890's, such events are still rare at this time. This is both due to the limited means of transport, and especially to the diversity of the rules applied. Each club has its own rules particularly regarding the size of the court, which in turn determine the number of players as well as the type of game played (heavy-hitting or a touch play).

The birth of the Badminton Association

The need for standardisation becomes more and more urgent. Accordingly, in August 1893 Major Seymour S.C. Dolby who is honorary secretary of the Southsea Club, writes to all the existing English clubs and to *The Field*. This newsletter calls for a meeting on 13th September at his "Dunbar" residence in Southsea, Hampshire, with the aim of setting up a "Badminton Association".

Nine clubs meet together and decide to create the Badminton Association (B.A.). Colonel S.S.C. Dolby is elected Honorary Secretary and Treasurer. Dolby, who was one of the first members of the Folkestone Army Officers club in 1875, moved to Southsea in 1890. He would remain at the head of the B.A. until 1899. In this year he would move to South Africa to participate in the Badminton boom and found the United Services Badminton Club in Wynberg, Cape Province.

Badminton develops throughout the British Isles

Badminton spreads quickly throughout certain parts of the British Isles. It is thanks to Dr McTier and other newly retired officers back from India that it gets a foothold in Scotland, at St. Andrews in the 1890's. The first club match is between St. Andrews and Aberdeen in 1900.

The first club in Ireland is in Limavady in 1892. Rapid expansion of the game in Ireland continues with clubs in Derry, Coleraine, and Wicklow. In November 1899, there is a meeting of several clubs in Dublin to create the Irish Badminton Union and to standardise the rules. As with the Badminton Association, the creation of the Irish union is a result of disagreement between the clubs notably Wicklow and Duncrum about how to organise matches. Colonel Gelston becomes honorary secretary.

However, despite Badminton becoming an organised and codified sport in Britain at the turn of the century, battledore and shuttlecock is not abandoned.

It continues to find representation in works of art in the late 19th century by Moore in England, Spinetti in Italy, Renoir and Denis in France. The press uses the medieval game during this period to illustrate political and military conflicts. In 1873, *The Popular Recreator* dispenses advice about how to go about making rackets to play "Battledore & shuttlecock". This is the same year that Badminton is first described in *The Field.*

Easy as it is to make a racket for the beginner, the article proposes how to make a racket with the head made out of two stretched parchments for the more advanced players : *"The next thing is to make the parchment head. it is to be cut to the shape of the spade, with a margin large enough to turn down over the woodwork and in this margin you must make notches, so that when turned down it may lie neatly. Soak the parchment in water, take off the damp, and glue it by the margin to the woodwork. Repeat this on the other side. To finish the handle, bind round it a slip of coloured velvet or leather. Now you have the battledore complete".*

However, two conditions are still necessary for a sport to achieve true notoriety. The first is the organisation of competitions and the second is for the sport to go beyond the borders of its country of origin. Competition and globalisation, dealt with in the next two chapters, would be the next stages in the game's development.

Kruger. — Les prisonniers anglais s'amusent à jouer au lawn-tennis... moi aussi !

PUNCH'S ESSENCE OF PARLIAMENT.

LIEBIG'S Fleisch-Extract.
Damen-Moden 1860.

LE VOLANT

Chapter 4 : Towards a Structured and Codified Sport

Now that it is an officially recognised sport with standardised rules and a national Association, Badminton is ready to develop further. In this respect, the increase in the number of competitions plays an important role.

On 10 March 1898, the first tournament is organised by the Guildford Badminton Club and patronised by Mr Percy Buckley. Twenty players register for the mixed doubles, six for the ladies doubles and seven for the men's doubles. Singles matches don't exist yet. Miss St John and D. Oakes win the mixed doubles while Mrs Cammell and Miss St John are victorious in the ladies doubles. D. Oakes and Stewart M. Massey win the men's doubles. The tournament is played on a waisted hourglass court.

Birth of the All-England Championships

As a result of the Guildford tournament's success, the first "Badminton Association Tournament" follows hot on its heels the following year. The competition takes place on one single day on 4th April. According to Stewart M. Massey (in his book *Badminton* published in 1911) the founders of the tournament that would become Badminton's "Wimbledon" are Messrs St Andrew St John, Buckley, Hart, Kelley, and Vidal.

The Championships sets up home at the London Scottish Drill Hall in London. There are four courts drawn out in chalk still using the hourglass shape. Three trophies could be won : the mens' and ladies' doubles, as well as the mixed doubles. If the winner is victorious three years running he or she can keep the trophy. Fifty-two players register for the Championships.

The first shuttlecocks used in competition are called "barrel shuttles" due to their shape. They comprise chicken's feathers inserted into the cork with the flat side of the quill facing outwards. The barrel shape is created by the natural curves of the feathers. The shuttlecock trajectory is already codified as *"a regular flight with less than 20-cm deviation over a distance of 13 metres"*. Goose feathers and other English products later replace the first shuttlecocks, with a straighter shape producing an optimised flight and speed.

The rackets on the other hand mainly come from Sealkot (India). As the game develops and the hitting becomes harder, there is a need for more solid rackets. The English equipment makers – Prosser, Jefferies and Slazengers – would compete with each other for the market.

In 1900, with 45 clubs now affiliated to the B.A., the first singles tournament is introduced to the Badminton Association Tournament. The first singles winners are Mr Sidney H. Smith and Miss Ethel Thompson. The matches are played up to 15 points.

1901 is an important date for the English tournament and for world Badminton in general. The rectangular court version is adopted, following an official request by General Shakespear of the Southsea Club. This, along with the abolition of handicap events and the reduction of ladies matches to 11 points, is the main innovation at the turn of the century.

In 1902, the tournament is called the "All-England Championships" and moves to the Crystal Palace Transept in Sydenham, Kent. Six courts are available for the 3-day event, *but "the light is poor and, shape of things to come, there is a distinct drift, a strong air-current that alters the shuttle's true-flight"*. The number of entries increases : 49 women and 47 men. For the first time, there are participants from as far as Scotland and Ireland. The matches are now played on six courts and over three days. Messrs H.I. Mellersh and F.S. Collier (Guildford Club), keep the trophy after three successive victories. The following year the tournament settles down at the London Rifle Brigade in Bunhill Row where it would remain until 1910.

Several innovations illustrate the rapidly increasing popularity of Badminton during the first decade of the 20th century. The first Badminton halls are built in Ealing to cope with the increase in the number of players and competitions. Then, there is the organisation of the first male veterans' championships in 1905 for over 45's. In 1907, the ladies' singles scoring changes from 15 points to 11 (*Lawn Tennis Badminton & Croquet*, April 3, 1907).

An increase in the number of tournaments played in the British Isles is also attested. H.H. Humfry is the enthusiast behind the first Irish National Championships the 3rd and 4th of February 1902 at Earlsfort Terrace Rink in Dublin.

In 1903, still in Dublin, the first international match occurs. The English defeat Ireland 5 - 2. Albert D. Prebble is England's captain while Stewart M. Massey who won the mens' doubles at the All-England Championships in 1899 and 1903 captains Ireland. The Scottish Championships follow in 1907 in Aberdeen on T.L. Adam's initiative.

The official Badminton magazine *The Badminton Gazette* is created in November 1907. Messrs Stewart M. Massey and George A. Thomas are successively the first editors. This magazine is launched on the initiative of C. Dudfield Willis and Albert D. Prebble after noticing that Badminton is hardly mentioned in the *Lawn-Tennis and Croquet* publication. The first issue of *The Badminton Gazette* states that *"Badminton has progressed so much in people's estimations that it will soon be as well known as Lawn-Tennis".*

Attempts to develop Badminton outside the United Kingdom

More and more tournaments, its own magazine, the building of halls, but also the start of the game's spread to other continents. During the beginning of the 20th century Badminton's progress is not only confined to Europe but also develops to a lesser extent in the Pacific and North America.

In 1900 the first matches are played in Freemantle, Australia, thanks to Mr Moore who brought back eight rackets from his holidays in Great Britain. The first Badminton club is set up in Montreal, Canada. Competitions are organised in Austria at the Viennese Park Club from the 1907-1908 season. The players come exclusively from the middle and upper classes : aristocrats, businessmen and people from the industrial sector.

An Englishman, J.E. Jones, is responsible for bringing the game to France in 1898. This British army coach builds four courts in Saint-Servan. This fact is confirmed in the chapter "The game in France" in Stewart M. Massey's book *Badminton* (1911) : *"Saint-Servan (seaside resort near St-Malo) seems to have been the first Badminton location in France. In 1898, Mr Jones, owner of a school and army coach, built four indoor Badminton courts for his students. However upon payment of a membership fee, his friends from Paramé and Saint-Servan could also use the club's facilities. The club prospered for six years but closed when Mr Jones left, unable to be managed by the local residents. A few courts survived however while some fans met once a week at a hotel in Paramé to play, notwithstanding a few obstacles including a chandelier in the middle of the room".*

Dieppe : pioneer city of French Badminton

An indoor Lawn-Tennis and Badminton club is set up in Dieppe on 31st October, 1907. One Tennis court and two Badminton courts are inaugurated in a certain Mr Meyer's garage. Night play is possible as there is electric lighting.

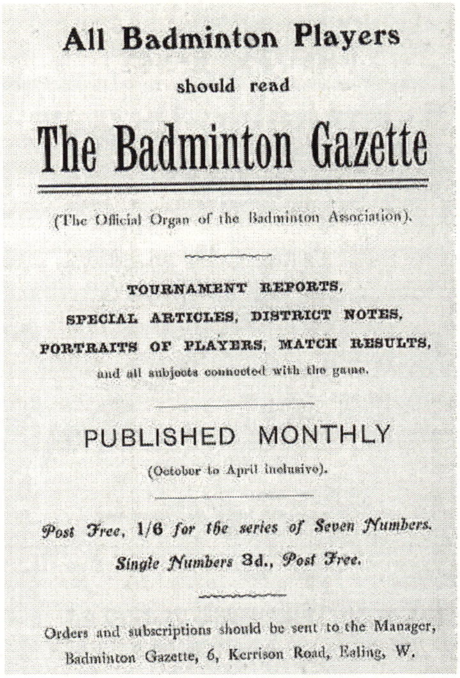

There are several reasons for the birth of French Badminton at Dieppe. It is a favourite holiday location for both British and Parisians. The railway link Paris-Dieppe is inaugurated in 1848 and built by English technicians and engineers. From 1870, sports, notably the "*Jeu de paume*", are very popular in this seaside resort. Winston Churchill plays golf there. The Prince of Wales and Oscar Wilde stay there on several occasions. At the turn of the century there is an English community of 3,000 people out of a total population of 25,000.

Charles Meyer, a Dane, arrives in Dieppe in 1888. A keen cyclist, he participates in many races. He wins Paris-Trouville-Paris, Paris – Royan, and the renowned Bordeaux – Paris races. He sets up a bike shop and devotes himself to automobiles. His garage is on the Place du Casino. His annex is in Thiers Street and is the location for the Dieppe Badminton Club's training sessions and tournaments. The site also is used for fencing, and roller-skating.

In 1908, the Dieppe Badminton Club organises the first competition outside the British Isles. This tournament follows the success of a series of challenger events including the unusual "three mix" event, competition opposing teams of two women and one man with matches up to 21 points. Planned for the beginning of the year the international event is postponed several times.

On October 2nd 1908, the club re-elects its Council. It comprises of Messrs Holl (president), Taylor (secretary), J. Yeo-Thomas (treasurer), and Major A.R.B. Savage (tournament organiser). The honorary members are particularly prestigious : Camille Coche, Mayor of Dieppe ; Henri-William Lee-Jortin, English Consul ; Walter Palmer-Samborne, English Proconsul.

The association, which has doubled its membership in a year, is officially declared on 23 November 1908. Its aim is to *"promote the love of Badminton"* through competitions and exhibition matches.

The Badminton Gazette encourages the Dieppe Club, the first to be created on the continent, supporting it as follows : *"The first open gathering outside of the British Isles constitutes an important step in the increasing popularity of Badminton and it is the duty of the game's fans to do all they can to ensure its success. Local enthusiasm and will-power is not lacking, but for the tournament objectives to be reached, it is indispensable that many British players take part. We note that the programme includes several events to allow competitors to play more games. Although the tournament starts on Friday, allowances will be made to English players unable to make the crossing before Friday evening".*

A few weeks prior to the opening of the International Tournament in Dieppe, the magazine insists on the necessary presence of English players. It specifies that all the conditions are satisfied and the hall can easily accommodate a thousand spectators.

One hundred and one entries are confirmed of which thirty are from the United Kingdom. Brimming with confidence, the secretary pleads the French players *"not to thrash the English players too much so that they return next year".*

Success of continental Europe's first international tournament

The matches start Friday November 27th and finish Sunday 29th. The first men's singles winner is the British player Frank Chesterton who after dominating Mr George A. Thomas in the semi-final beats his compatriot Mr H. Comyn in the final 15-11, 15-9. The ladies' champion is Miss Margaret Rivers Larminie who easily beats Mrs W. Taylor of the Dieppe Club 11-1, 11-6. The presentation of the trophies is made in the presence of the English association's secretary Mr C. Dudfield-Willis.

The local press is full of praise for *"this tournament which housed some very tight and exciting matches"*. In a separate article, the game of Badminton is enthused over for its capacity to bring together English and French in a common pastime : *"Not so long ago, players from our town who were looking for a means of entertainment to fill the long and monotonous winter days created the game of Badminton. This was a good idea ; it established itself quickly. An association was founded and gradually members joined in numbers. Today, the Dieppe Badminton Club is very prosperous and gathers together large sections of the English community and all the elite of Dieppe society..."*

The London newspapers are not to be outdone : *"Last week the first Badminton Open took place in France. This event was organised by the Dieppe B.C. and was held in the magnificent garage of Mr Meyer (the runner up in the men's singles by handicap and a true sportsman) who generously put his hall at the committee's disposal... The Dieppe Club whose members include French, British, and Americans, is run by the president, Mr M.S. Holl"*.

The author of this article, Stewart Massey, himself a participant in the open tournament, makes an analysis of the French players' game : *"So far this newly-opened club has had the handicap of not having seen the game's top players in action. Bearing this in mind, the level they have reached is very good and several players already show excellent skills... Their game however currently lacks edge. They play too defensively instead of attacking. In Badminton attack is the best form of defence. The Dieppe players' serving was perhaps the best part of their game. As soon as they have learnt to execute the smash their game will double in efficiency. It was very apparent how the Dieppe players played better when facing a British opponent. Their game in these conditions acquired another dimension"*.

The DBC, basking in the glow of this success, and *"wishing to spread the enthusiasm for this exciting game"* travels to the outskirts of Paris on 7th February 1909, to play exhibition matches at the Neuilly-sur-Seine Tennis Club. The hall was gracefully provided by Mr Little (Williams Company). *The Badminton Gazette* would cover the event : *"If Badminton doesn't catch on in France, it won't be the fault of the Dieppe players whose enthusiasm was there for all to see. Max Decugis, A. Germot and many other Tennis stars were present at the matches. One can add that this exhibition attracted the Parisian press' full attention"*.

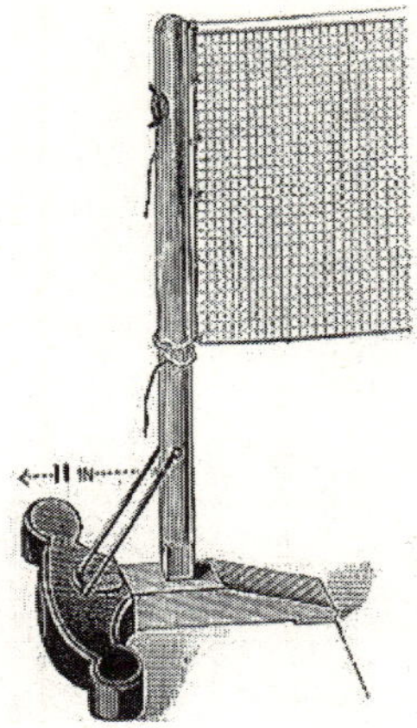

The event's impact is nevertheless limited in terms of the development of the game outside of Dieppe. At the end of 1909, there is new hope however in the form of J. Yeo-Thomas' departure for Paris : *"If the game hasn't completely caught on in the French capital, his arrival will bring new impetus to the movement"* (*Badminton Gazette*).

The second "French Open" organised in December 1909 receives 70 entries. Once again Mr Frank Chesterton beats George A. Thomas in the final. However there is French success in the mixed doubles with handicap thanks to the pair Charles Meyer and Mrs W. Taylor. On behalf of his friends, George A. Thomas thanks their French hosts for the warmest of welcomes and compliments the DBC *"for having created the system of school subscriptions, the best means of recruitment and propaganda"*.

The main international tournament however, despite the efforts of the DBC, is the All-England Championships held at the Horticultural hall in Westminster from 1910. The Scottish and the Irish take advantage of this event to play their first international tournament that year.

Modernisation and expansion of Badminton

As for the equipment, it becomes more and more sophisticated. A shuttle-testing machine is first used at the 1908 tournament. But it has the annoying habit of breaking the racket handles used to strike it : *"an unrealised dream"* according to Sir George Thomas in 1957 in *The Badminton Gazette…*

In 1911 in England, Stewart M. Massey writes *Badminton*, the first book entirely devoted to the game. The book deals with the game's history, the rules, the results of the big tournaments and the equipment used.

The publication of this reference book on the subject illustrates the game's rise in popularity : accordingly, it increases from 27 clubs in 1897 to 325 in 1911. The exchanges between France and England continue. Following the British players' participation in the French open, the DBC receives the London club Ealing in 1913. The French are given a lesson in the art of Badminton : the English win 102 sets to Dieppe's 45.

The rise of Badminton, thanks to the Anglo-French collaboration, is stopped in its tracks by the outbreak of the First World War. The war interrupts the "golden age" of Badminton, particularly in France where the Dieppe enclave would remain isolated from the rest of the country.

However, whereas before the war the sport is confined to the British Isles and a few European enclaves, after the Great War it would be exported to other parts of the globe.

Chapter 5 : Spreading the Passion for Badminton

The development of Badminton is interrupted by the outbreak of the First World War. This not only leads to the competitions being suspended, but also to a clean break from the amateur spirit that has accompanied the game's evolution before the war.

Betty Uber, a many-times winner of the All-England Championships in both singles and doubles and inspiration behind the famous "Uber Cup", will regret this change in the spirit with which the game is played in her book *That Badminton Racket* : *"One feature of the game before 1914, and I think for some few years after the war, was the fact that it was a purely amateur game, in the real sense of the words. In its very early days it was played exclusively by the Services, then later, after developing, by people who had sufficient income and sufficient leisure to enable them to travel about and become members of clubs. I do not think it had occurred to any-one that it might be possible to make big money or indeed any money at all, out of the game. Badminton was so little known that except for one's own*

satisfaction there was nothing to be gained in a financial or commercial way by being a champ".

Post-war problems resuming Badminton competitions

The old habit of meeting to play Badminton is slow to take off after the war. The next All-England Championships are held only in 1920. This is partly explained by the difficulty in finding available halls and good quality shuttlecocks. There is a shortage of courts for a while as the drill halls are only gradually released for peacetime use. Shuttles are scarce because the upheavals in Europe have affected the supply of goose feathers.

The post-war Championships are dominated by 40 year old Sir George A. Thomas who wins four consecutive titles from 1920 to 1923. Due to quite exceptional longevity he would also be able to win the mens' doubles at the age of 48. He also participated in the Wimbledon Tennis Championships reaching the semi-finals of the men's doubles in 1911 as well as being a member of the English chess team. In the 1930's he would become a distinguished leader of the Badminton Association and later President of the International Badminton Federation (from 1934 to 1955).

The ladies game also has its dominant figure in the 1920's in the form of Kitty McKane. She wins several AEC titles in mixed doubles and with her sister in the ladies' doubles, as well as the singles. In 1920, she is victorious at both the AEC (Badminton) and Wimbledon (Tennis).

A lot of famous players at this time come from one of the three big London clubs : Crystal Palace, Alexandra Palace and Logan. Ealing and Richmond also provide strong competition.

The dominant Irish model

Surprisingly however, it is Ireland that provides Badminton with the greatest champions between the wars. G.S.B. "Curly" Mack wins the AEC in 1924 before being succeeded by J. Frank Devlin (six singles titles from 1925 to 1931). Born in Dublin, Devlin would win a total of 18 AEC titles before turning professional in 1931, much to the relief of his long-suffering opponents. The success of Irish Badminton at this time owes much to two of its most prominent figures : J. Plunkett-Dillon (Irish team manager) and Major J.D.M. McCallum (founder of a wandering team called "The Strollers" whose vocation is to promote the game of Badminton).

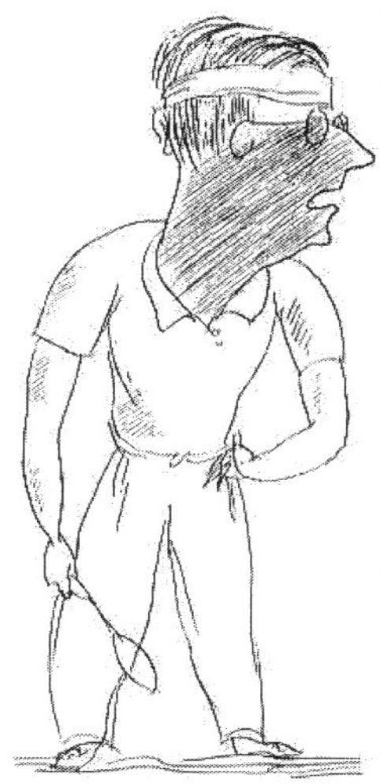

The popularity of the AEC – held since 1910 at the Horticultural hall in Westminster – spreads fast and at the same time British Badminton carries on developing. Each year fifty new clubs are affiliated to the Badminton

Association. Other associations and regional championships increase in numbers. It is Scotland's turn to establish itself as an important centre for the game thanks to the beneficial effects of the Scottish National Championships. In 1922, Scotland plays and loses (0-9) its first international meeting against the best team in the world : England. In Wales, Trevor Williams founds the Welsh Badminton Union (January 1928).

In the 1920's, the game's Rules are further developed. Certain Rules are clarified (double-hitting, obstruction) and the Badminton Association in 1921 raises the question of professionalism with an initial definition. Among its stipulation is that anyone who *"has competed against a professional, has accepted expenses from a body other than the Badminton Association or is a professional in other branch of sport"* must be defined as a professional. But the B.A. Committee decides that it's *"not necessary or desirable at the present time to frame any definition of a professional in their rules*". Members consider that it is better to deal with future cases individually.

The fact that this question is raised more and more and at the highest level testifies that tournament prizes, sponsorships and travel indemnities are becoming unavoidable issues.

The inter-war period is characterised by the spread of Badminton beyond the British Isles.

Surge of Badminton in Denmark

Firstly, Badminton begins to take roots in Northern Europe. An irresistible surge is observable in Holland. A British team composed of Messrs R.M. "Bill" White and Ian Maconachie and Miss Kingsbury and Mrs Betty Uber, perform at Rotterdam, Amsterdam, and The Hague.

Badminton's development is even more pronounced in Denmark where in the space of a few years it has become a national sport producing players of the highest level *"adopting it as a national winter sport, setting up good facilities from the start and organising themselves so well that in just over a decade they have produced an All-England champion"* (B. Adams).

The origins of Danish Badminton can be traced to 1925 in a gymnasium north of Copenhagen following an initiative by four Tennis players wishing to diversify their sports activities. These four players are invited to give an exhibition match in front of six spectators on 10th September 1925. The pioneers of the new Danish national sport are Schrader, Hansen, Olsen and Nexoe-Larsen.

As well as the Hansen brothers' exhibition matches, The Strollers' tour of Denmark would be responsible for increasing Badminton's audience. Major McCallum's British team, at the peak of its form, wins all its matches against its Danish counterparts in 1929. However, this tour would be of great benefit to Danish Badminton with a National Badminton Association being created, as well as a steady increase in the number of players, the building of Badminton halls and the number of international meetings. The Strollers would return to Denmark the following year and in 1933 to continue with the promotion of Danish Badminton. Danish Badminton would achieve its first major success in 1935 beating Wales 3-2 in the presence of Prince Axel of Denmark and before an audience of fifteen hundred.

In addition to becoming one of the sport's major nations, the Danes would also make a big contribution to the game's growing success in Sweden. The Hansen brothers make a tour of Sweden in 1933 and perform exhibition matches in the presence of King Gustave.

In 1939, Tage Madsen confirms Denmark's influence in European Badminton by winning the AEC mens' singles, the first success in the Championships by a Danish player.

Badminton boom in Canada and the USA

Badminton also develops quickly in North America. In Canada, the Canadian Badminton Association is created in December 1921. This Association is the fulfilment following a soar in the game's popularity that has already overseen the Ladies' Montreal Tennis and Badminton Club in 1907 as well as the first open tournament in 1914.

At the instigation of the CBA president Colonel McKee, the first Canadian National Championships hold the following year in Montreal. In 1925 the CBA invites a powerful English team to promote the sport further. Led by Sir George A. Thomas, the team includes Frank Devlin, Jones, Hawthorn, Martin and Swinden. The tour lasts three weeks from coast to coast with the exhibitions revealing the significant gap existing between the two nations.

Five years later, a second tour is organised again with Sir George A. Thomas as captain. A match is held at the Granite Club in Toronto with England winning 7-2. The best Canadian player, Jack Purcell defeats Donald Hume. In *The Badminton Gazette*, Frank Devlin praises the Canadians for their progress not only for their sports performances but also for their playing conditions : *"it is difficult to imagine the wonderful playing conditions existing in Canada, and one must go there to realise what it is like to play in an hall specially built for the game, with attention paid to the many etceteras such as dressing-rooms, lounges and catering arrangements. All the buildings are heated, but the actual courts are kept at 50° F, and in the ordinary way spectators sit in the warm and watch the game through enormous plate glass windows".*

In 1931, Jack Purcell participates in the AEC confirming the growing international dimension to both the English tournament and the game of Badminton. Holder of the Canadian Championships in 1927, from the town of Toronto, Purcell "the cat" reaches the semi-finals only to be beaten by T.P. Dick. Canada's first taste of glory in the championships is in 1939 with Mrs Dorothy Walton's victory in the AEC ladies' singles.

New York is the starting point for the history of Badminton in the USA. In 1878 the New Yorkers, Bayard Clarke and E. Langdon, return from India and England respectively. They had discovered the new game of Badminton. Along with one of their friends, Oakley Rhinelander, they decide to create the New York Badminton Club. Initially perceived as a social pastime, regular matches are nevertheless played at the New York and Boston clubs, the latter being created in 1908.

From the 1920's, Badminton spreads throughout the country. American Badminton rapidly seeks contacts with other nations. In 1924, the honorary secretary of the Boston Club, Dr. Cannes, goes to Canada to sell the idea of an international match based on the already-famous Davis Cup Tennis tournament. But this initiative would only be fully realised 30 years later with the creation of the "Thomas Cup". In 1925, the English team finishes its North America tour in New York.

The game's blossoming in the USA is also a result of exhibitions by the professional George Jess Willard, particularly appreciated by the Hollywood community. In 1935 in Seattle, Jess Willard plays Jack Purcell in front of

3,000 spectators. The latter wins in 3 sets. Jess Willard and Bill Hurley subsequently would travel through America for three months performing exhibitions in front of a million people and thus rendering inevitable the creation of a real national association.

Ken Davidson, a brilliant Scottish player, settles down in New York in November 1935 and also contributes to the promotion of Badminton with his own unique and amusing style.

On the 28 June, 1936, the American Badminton Association is formed and the first national championships would be held in Chicago the following year. In the 1939 open, a young 18 year-old player takes the game by storm. David Freeman from Pasadena surprises observers by defeating the defending champion Walter Kramer. His supremacy lasts a decade, albeit interrupted by the Second World War, and culminates with the AEC mens' singles title in 1949.

Gradual progression of Asian Badminton

In Asia, Badminton's development is slower and more targeted.

In India for a long time, it has been a popular game played outside. However, the first indoor tournament is not organised before 1929 in Punjab. The first All-India Championships take place in 1934 revealing talents of players such as Devinda Mohan and Prakash Nath in the 1940's.

The Malayan States benefit from the experience of the English military of the East India Company, as well as impetus given by the Anglican and Methodist missionaries who associate Badminton with the development of the body and the spirit. The Penang Badminton Association is created in 1925. Penang, Selangor, Perak, Johore and Singapore meet to form the Malayan Badminton Association in 1934. Devlin makes a tour there in 1937 noting that the Malayans have two important assets, their speed and their ability to learn quickly. By the following year, 25,000 Malayans are recorded to be regularly playing the game.

In Australasia, the growth of Badminton affects New Zealand first. A first club, the Auckland Badminton Club is created in 1900. The New Zealand Championships are inaugurated in 1927 in Wanganui. In the same year the New Zealand Badminton Association is founded. Just before the war (1938) a first international match would be organised between Australia and New Zealand for the "Whyte Trophy".

Faced with such enthusiasm for the game and its rapid geographical expansion there is urgent need for union and harmony in the game on a global scale.

Creation of an international Federation

On the 5th July 1934, representatives from all the known national Federations meet in the Aldwych, London, with the aim of forming an international Federation. Messrs Colonel R. Bruce Hay, B.L. Bisgood and A.D. Prebble represent the Badminton Association.

The participating countries are : Canada (Mr Hollings), Denmark (Messrs van Vossen and Speaighy), Holland (Mr den Hoed), Ireland (Messrs Plunkett Dillon and Major McCallum), Scotland (Messrs Gibson and Millar), New Zealand (Mr Andrews), Wales (Messrs Hughes and Williams). France, despite the slow down in its Badminton boom after the First World War and the fact that it is still only confined to a few towns, is also represented in the form of Mr René Gathier. England has five representatives : Sir George A. Thomas, E. Hawthorn, D.L.H. Mercer, G.E. Mills and L.T. Wickham.

A.D. Prebble presides over the meeting. After a preliminary description of the history of Badminton, he announces that the time has come to entrust the management of fundamental Badminton laws to an international organisation. A decision is taken to create the International Badminton Federation (IBF). Sir George Thomas is elected President. F.W. Hickson becomes General Secretary with an official address : 74 Grange Drive, Winchmore Hill, London.

The creation of the IBF constitutes an important stage in the history of Badminton. It emphasises both its true international dimension – even if some countries are still absent : US, India, Malaya – and a certain distancing from the historically influential Badminton Association.

The first champions' promotion compensates for modest media coverage

However, in the same year 1934, there is concern at the lack of importance given by the media to the Badminton events. In fact, radio and newspaper only start showing interest in the sport in the late 1930's : a lengthy and well-informed article appears in *The Evening Standard* in May 1938 ; the BBC commentates 15 minutes of an AEC match in 1937.

Important as this first media coverage is, Badminton's popularity is largely thanks to its great champions. Numerous books on Badminton appear in the 20's and 30's. Generally written by ex-players, these manuals are essentially of a technical nature describing how best to hit, or move around the court. They also cover the tactical side of the game and expose in detail the games basic rules. The following players swap racket for pen to recount their experiences and provide educational works for the next generations of players : Sir George A. Thomas (*The Art of Badminton*, 1923), G.S.B. "Curly" Mack (*Badminton*, 1925), Ferrers-Nicholson and Hedges *(The Art of Badminton*, 1934), Frank Devlin in 1936 with *Badminton for all* and finally Jackson and Swan in 1939 with *Better Badminton*).

In the late thirties, new stars appear on the world Badminton stage : Donald Hume (one AEC title), Bill White (two titles), Ralph Nichols (five titles), dominate the pre-war decade in the men's game. *"Ralph Nichols was perhaps the best all-rounder player of his particular time. His great attribute was a marvellous supple wrist but he was also grimly accurate and an astute reader of a match"* (B. Adams). As for the women's game, Mrs F.G. Barrett, the Kingsbury sisters, Thelma and Leoni, Mrs Betty Uber, Mrs Violet Elton and Mrs Marjorie Henderson share most of the spoils between them during this period.

These victories tend to indicate total and eternal domination by the English. However, victories at the 1939 AEC by the Dane Tage Madsen and the Canadian Dorothy Walton would prove to be the beginning of a new era for world Badminton. In fact, the Second World War announces the end of British domination of this sport.

CHURCHMAN'S CIGARETTES.
MEL
SIR GEORGE
A. THOMAS, BART.

The art of
Badminton
By
Mrs N. Ferrers-Nicholson
and
Sid G. Hedges

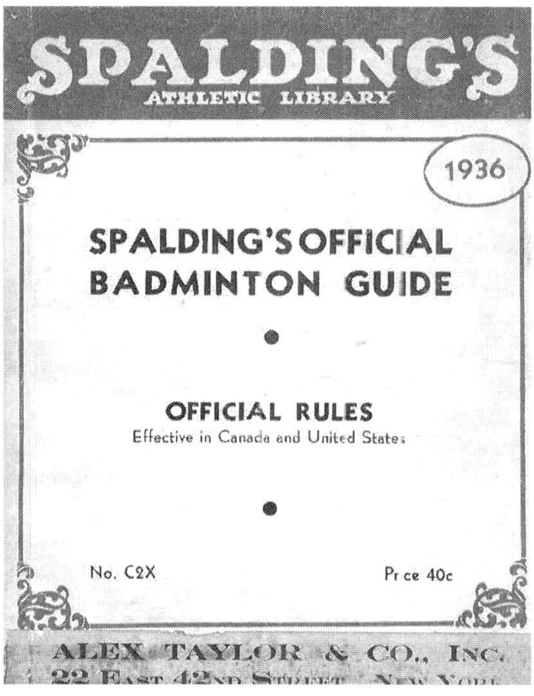
SPALDING'S
ATHLETIC LIBRARY
1936
SPALDING'S OFFICIAL
BADMINTON GUIDE
OFFICIAL RULES
Effective in Canada and United States
No. C2X
Price 40c
ALEX TAYLOR & CO., INC.

One good serve deserves ano
WED
·IN·THE·
WOOD
OLD
THOMPSON
BRAND

"You really uncorked a winner that time, Jim!"
Paul Jones
FIRST OF ALL...
FOR FLAVOR!

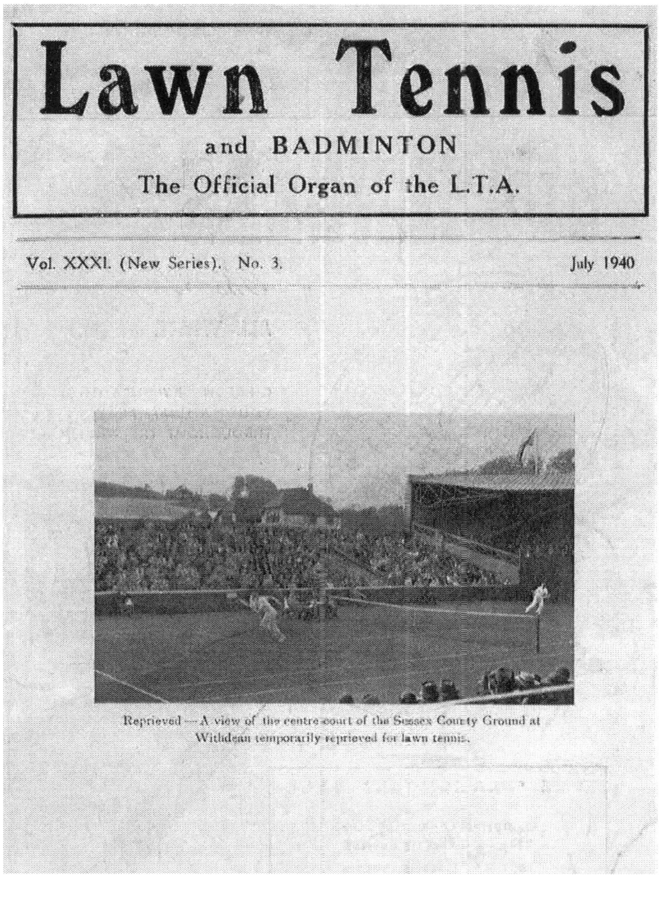

Lawn Tennis

and BADMINTON

The Official Organ of the L.T.A.

Vol. XXXI. (New Series). No. 3. July 1940

Reprieved — A view of the centre court of the Sussex County Ground at Withdean temporarily reprieved for lawn tennis.

Chapter 6 : Badminton Goes East

During the Second World War, Badminton is far from everybody's minds, especially in Europe. Even after the ceasefire, games do not resume normally immediately.

This is the case in England. Despite the existence of 1,500 clubs throughout the country in 1946, equipment – especially shuttlecocks – and halls are scarce : *"The war in Europe ended eighteen months ago, and yet a vast number of halls are still cluttered up with various official and unofficial belongings"* (*The Gazette*). The great club Logan, whose courts were used as storage areas during the war, would never again recover its former glory. Only Wimbledon continues to prosper as before uniting the majority of England's greatest players.

Post-war transport is still not fully re-established making it difficult for players to travel to tournaments. Hotels also encounter problems heating the rooms and providing enough food for a whole weekend of competition.

Betty Uber recalls resuming competitive play in the spring of 1946 in Littlehampton.

Similarly, even if the AEC finally resumes in March 1947, the conditions are difficult for players and spectators alike due to the lack of fuel and food. Snow even manages to disturb the first day of the 1947 tournament : "*it was not just a simple matter of sweeping it away because the wooden floor had been laid over an ice rink and the snow immediately froze ; it also meant that there was no heating in the hall anyway so on the first day of the tournament only six out of the sixty or seventy scheduled matches were completed*" (Brian Adams).

Denmark dominates European Badminton

The war has certainly prevented the young generation of British players from developing their skills in the footsteps of their predecessors. This is to the profit of the Danes who had been able to continue playing during the conflict. So the Danes sweep the board at the immediate post-war competitions. This new trend is confirmed in the 1948 meeting between the two leading countries in Copenhagen, with a glorious 6-1 victory for Denmark.

In the AEC, the Danes would win several titles : Jorn Skaarup in the singles (1948), Tage Madsen and Poul Holm (1947), Preben Dabelsteen and Borge Frederiksen (1948), and Dabelsteen and Skaarup (1950) in the men's doubles. Danish domination is even more flagrant in the ladies' events, winning all the singles between 1947 and 1953 as well as the doubles three years running 1950-1952. This success can be explained by several factors : investment in halls and facilities, very young players in Badminton clubs, strict national organisation.

To attempt to compete with the Danes, the Badminton Association decides to create a tournament for the under 18's. The first All-England Junior Championships are held in 1950. This new event helps the blossoming of young talent such as F. John Shaw and Tony Jordan into mens' champions, or June R. White and Heather M. Ward into ladies' champions. The hope for renewed British superiority would return in 1953 with June White and Iris Cooley's victory in the doubles.

Malaya's post-war superiority

On the world stage however, Asia is about to dominate both British and Danes in international competitions. At first this domination is Malayan with victories in the fifties. Wong Peng Soon (4 AEC singles titles) and Ewe Beng "Eddy" Choong (4 titles) – nicknamed the "Penang prodigy" - impress observers by their speed and dexterity. The Malayans follow on the footsteps of the Indians who had given the impression during the post war period of being on the verge of dominating world Badminton with players of the calibre of Mohan and Nath. *"They showed us a game which was different. Tremendously fast on their feet, they had a wonderful delicacy of touch and also made use to a great extent of deceptive play"* (Betty Uber). The latter would only lose to the Swedish Conny Jepsen in the final of the 1947 AEC.

The Indians indeed defeat the Danes 2-1 in 1948 in an epic meeting of the two countries. Malaya's supremacy would be confirmed with the organisation of the first world team competition for men.

This idea is in fact the brainchild of Sir George Thomas. In 1939, he made an official proposal at the IBF meeting on March 11. The idea was accepted by the General Assembly on 5th July 1939 and Sir George A. Thomas offered to donate a trophy. He presented the trophy – later to be called the "Thomas Cup" – to the IBF representatives in July 1940. But due to the war, this event was postponed until 1949.

The right to participate in the competition finals has to be gained via qualifiers divided into geographical zones. There are three zones : Pacific, North America and Europe. The matches are the best of nine, five singles and four doubles. The finals take place on the soil of the defending nation. The championships would be spread over three years.

The First "Thomas Cup" Tournament

Ten countries are on the starting blocks. In the European section, Denmark beats England 9-0, after England's victory over France by the same score. This result confirms the Danish players' recent domination of European Badminton. The USA beat Canada 8-1 and therefore gain the right to meet Malaya, winner of the Pacific zone play-offs, in Glasgow in February 1950.

The emergence of USA Badminton is hardly surprising given the vigour of its pre-war development. This is also due to the talent of its champion David Freeman who, according to the press, has not been beaten in an official tournament for ten years : *"He had most perfect footwork, and an*

ability to play shots that were perfectly produced in the classical style. Above all, he had a calm infinite patience in his singles games which in the end defeated all his opponents" (Betty Uber). Despite winning all his matches, David Freeman cannot prevent a Malayan victory (6-3) in front of 3,000 spectators at the Kelvin Hall in Glasgow.

The final is therefore played between Malaya and Denmark. The matches are played at the Queen's Hall in Preston, Lancashire. Thanks to their doubles pairings and despite an injury incurred by their leader Wong Peng Soon, the Malayans win the first ever Thomas Cup by 8 matches to 1. As a spectator, Betty Uber recalls that the Malayan players *"have shown us something new and different. They have developed their own way of hitting the bird, very much their own method of defence, and they show a speed of eye and footwork which is incredible to us. One of the main differences is that the shuttle at the moment of impact is about a foot further in front of the body than it would be with the orthodox English style. This gives the effect of a kind of hammer shot, which, although not so good to look at, seems wonderfully effective. It's difficult to see whether they were clearing or*

dropping, both actions being the same and the final intention being very well disguised" (Betty Uber).

In Torquay the same year, a friendly match between Malaya and England results in an emphatic 9-0 victory for the Malayans. In the All-England Championships of the same year, 1950, Malaya wins the men's doubles with the pairing Ooi Teik Hock and Teoh Seng Khoon. This is despite the presence of other great Badminton nations (USA, Sweden, India) making half of the 46 overseas entries. Malayan supremacy in world Badminton is confirmed.

Indeed, they would continue this supremacy throughout the fifties. Following numerous successes in the AEC's between 1950 and 1956 at the Empress Hall in Earl's Court, the Malayans would successfully defend the Thomas Cup three years later.

The first matches start in 1951. For the European zone, France is beaten 9-0 again by England in Paris, despite their attempts to reverse the trend by establishing a central Badminton commission within the French Lawn-Tennis Federation. Among the 20 other teams competing two teams stand out : Malaya and the USA. These two teams indeed meet in the final for the second Thomas Cup. In an atmosphere of indescribable enthusiasm and intense heat of Singapore, the Malayans retain their trophy.

In 1955, for the third Championships, the Malayans play Denmark again in the final. The score is an emphatic 8-1 victory for the Asians. However, a new rival to their supremacy seems to be emerging at this time in the form of Indonesia. At the Malayan Open, a young Indonesian from Java, Ferry Sonneville, beats champion Wong Peng Soon in three sets. This victory symbolises the emergence of the Indonesians into world Badminton. For their first participation in the Thomas Cup (1958), they successively defeat Denmark (6-3) and Malaya (6-3), the latter in front of their home supporters. This is the first in a long series of seven victories in the team event for Indonesia, only interrupted by the Malaysian's victory in 1967.

The creation of the "Uber Cup"

The success of the Thomas Cup is not without repercussions on the ladies sport. The ladies have been omnipresent in world Badminton since the beginning – indeed the ladies' doubles existed before the mens' singles at the AEC. The time has come for the ladies to play in a team competition equivalent to the Thomas Cup for the men.

Helped by her international fame, Betty Uber proposes the creation of a team tournament for ladies in 1950. She finds support in the form of New Zealand's Nancy Fleming. For financial reasons, the competition's organisation is put off until 1955 when Mrs Uber presents a trophy and the official decision to launch the event is taken by the IBF.

Eleven nations register for the first "Uber Cup". The final, played at Lytham St Annes in England, brings together the USA and Denmark. Despite dominating ladies world Badminton in the early fifties with players such as Mrs Aase Jacobsen, Mrs Tonny Ahm and Mrs Marie Ussing, Denmark soon concedes supremacy to America. In 1954, Judy Devlin, 18 years old, won the AEC singles, the first of five US victories shared with her compatriot Margaret Varner in the 1950's.

Thanks to its two champions, the USA wins the first Uber Cup 6-1. They would go on to win the next two Uber Cup events as well, before losing the title to the Japanese and Indonesians in the mid sixties.

The successes acquired by the Asians in the major international competitions, the Thomas Cup, the Uber Cup and the AEC's, would lead to two important initiatives for Asian Badminton. In 1959, the Asian Badminton Confederation (ABC) is created on the instigation of the Malayan Federation. Three years later, the first Asian tournament is organised at the Negara Stadium, Kuala Lumpur.

Still in 1962, Badminton is officially introduced at the Asian games (inaugurated in 1949 by Afghanistan, Burma, India, Pakistan and the Philippines). The Games would take place in Jakarta, Indonesia, a year after winning its second Thomas Cup.

In the sixties and seventies, Indonesia and Malaysia dominate the men's sport ; Japan, USA, Denmark and England the ladies.

The success of the Thomas and Uber Cup competitions, the conquest of new territories (China, Thailand, and South Korea) and the increase in the number of players in the world should logically lead to the game's rapid ascension to Olympic status.

However, after several unsuccessful attempts and various political and sporting changes, it would be necessary to wait until the Barcelona Olympics in 1992 for Badminton to reach full maturity and its first Olympic gold medal to be awarded.

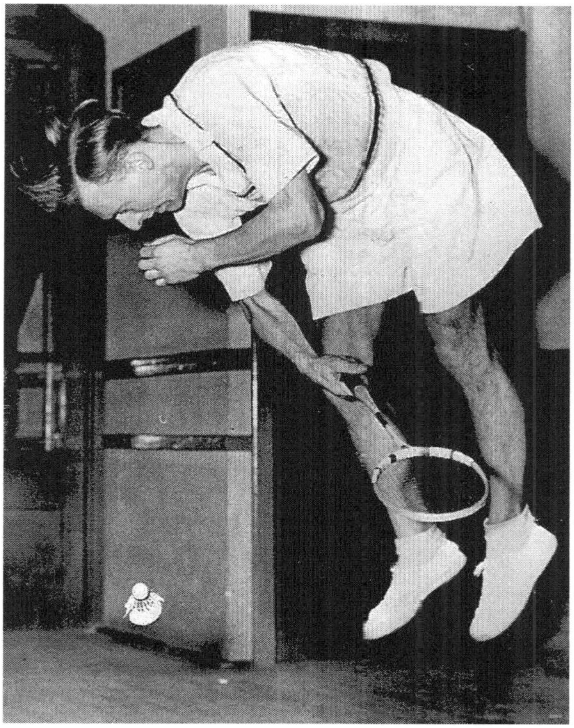

U.S.A.

Chapter 7 :
The Long and Difficult Path to Olympic Status

At the beginning of the seventies, Badminton seems ready to be integrated into the greatest sports event of the planet : the Olympic Games.

The future of Badminton is secure with the All-England Championships inaugurated in 1899 and the Thomas and Uber Cups flourishing since the fifties.

China wakes up

The number of countries affiliated to the IBF continues growing. The number of players rockets with the arrival of China on the international scene even if it cannot be a member of the IBF for the time being as Taiwan is already a member.

In 1965, the Chinese team visits its Danish counterparts and causes a storm by winning all of its 24 singles matches. Strict and new training methods based on running and jumping, supple wrist technique, and unprecedented team discipline seem to be the recipes for success.

The Chinese are back in Europe in 1973 for a tour of England : London, Bristol, Carlisle and Birmingham. Some matches take place in front of up to 2,000 people. The English would return the compliment the following year for a series of friendly matches.

The Chinese quickly establish themselves in this new sports event. At the Asian Games in Tehran in 1974, the Chinese team beats the great Indonesian team, holder of the Thomas Cup for the previous two meetings. Badminton would find a structure in Asia thanks to the creation of the ABC and the sport's integration into the Asian Games.

In North America, the organisers opt for using the same methods as those used to promote Badminton in Asia : Badminton is included in the 8th Commonwealth Games held in Jamaica (1966) ; it is also decided to create an annual competition between mixed teams from the USA and Canada. This new tournament is baptised the “Devlin Cup” as a tribute to the famous Irish player J. Frank Devlin.

In Europe too, in an attempt to improve Badminton’s image, decisions are taken to increase the number of major continental events. In 1962 in Zurich, the “Helvetia Cup” brings together the weakest European teams for a tournament. West Germany wins ten years running (1962-1971). In September 1967, the European Badminton Union is founded. The Swiss H.P. Kunz is nominated president. At first, the EBU comprises Austria, Belgium, Czechoslovakia, Denmark, England, Finland, West Germany, Netherlands, Norway, Sweden and Switzerland. The following year it would expand to include France, Scotland, Ireland, Wales and Slovenia. Hungary (1973), the USSR (1974), and Italy (1977) would later also join the union.

Thanks to the personal intervention of H. Brohl and of Stellan Mohlin (ex-Swedish champion, member of the IBF Council, and future President of the European Badminton Union), a first European Championships is organised in Bochum, West Germany, in 1968. Sture Johnsson (Sweden) in the men's tournament and Irmgard Latz (West Germany) for the ladies are the first two players to have their names on the honours list of this new tournament.

In the wake of these European Championships, the EBU creates a junior European tournament to help the emergence of talented young players with the first tournament held in Voorburg (Holland). Finally, a team competition reserved for European teams is pioneered in 1972 to increase international meetings and, of course, prepare the European teams as well as possible for the formidable challenge awaiting them against their Asian and North American rivals. The English who beat the Danes in the final win the first European Team Championships, in which a total of twelve nations participate. This event would be held every two years with the English and Danes sharing the spoils and contesting European supremacy.

First attempt at Olympic status

1972 remains a turning point in the history of Badminton. The sport is included in the Munich Olympics as a demonstration sport. Among the 7,000 athletes competing at the games, 25 Badminton players are given the responsibility of promoting the qualities of Badminton. The Indonesian Rudy Hartono wins the mens' singles. The Indonesians are also victorious in the doubles thanks to Ade Chandra and Christian Hadinata. In the ladies events, only the singles is played and it is the Japanese player Noriko Nakayama who is crowned. The Europeans' consolation is a victory in the mixed doubles pairing of Derek Talbot and Gillian Gilks (GB).

Strengthening of the sport's regional organisation

In the wake of the Olympic inclusion, international competitions increase. In 1973, "La Plume d'Or" has the aim of gathering the so-called "small" Badminton nations such as France, Belgium, Portugal and Czechoslovakia. The first event is held in Verstoep, Brussels. The participating nations would meet on a yearly basis thereafter.

Three years later in 1976, the Pan-American Badminton Federation is founded mainly thanks to the tireless efforts of the Mexican V.J. Villalobos. Canada, the USA, and Mexico are among the tournament's founders as well as smaller nations like Trinidad and Tobago.

In 1977, the African continent takes an interest in Badminton. The African Badminton Association is created at the instigation of Nigeria. Ghana, Mauritius, Mozambique, Kenya, and Tanzania are the other founding members.

In the same year, the first World Badminton Championships are held in Malmo, Sweden. Until then, the All-England Championships have acted as the unofficial world tournament. However in 1975, the IBF decides that it is time to create a real "World Championships" distinct from the prestigious English event, and plan the first tournament for two years later. In the mens' and ladies' singles, the Danes, who are virtually playing at home, win thanks to Fleming Delfs and Lene Koppen respectively. In the mens' doubles the Indonesian pair Tjun Tjun and Wahjudi confirms for a second time their supremacy already displayed in the Thomas Cup.

With all these international representative bodies (ABC, ABF, EBU...) and the success of the different existing competitions (Thomas and Uber Cups, World Championships, Asian Games, Helvetia Cup...), Badminton's accession to the Olympic games seems just a matter of time. However a political division would postpone this well-deserved inclusion by more than a decade.

From political conflict to sports breakaway

On the 24th February 1978, thirteen Asian and six African associations meet in Hong Kong at the request of the Malaysian, Teh Gin Sooi. They agree to found the World Badminton Federation (WBF). In other words, these nations decide to split with the organisation running world Badminton since 1934, the IBF.

There are four major reasons behind this breakaway, which would have heavy consequences for Badminton's prestige and Olympic recognition. Firstly, the WBF's dissatisfaction is based on the refusal to expel Taiwan to allow the People's Republic of China to join the IBF. Given its size and importance, and the steady increase in the excellence of its players, China has been requesting admittance for some time. Secondly, the breakaway nations back the principle of "one nation, one vote" for the decision-making process. In addition, they refuse to ratify the existence of several British associations (England, Scotland, Ireland and Wales). Finally, they are against the inclusion of South Africa.

This new entity immediately puts in place a selective "World Championship" and calls for a boycott of both the All-England Championships and the Thomas Cup.

Faced with a potentially suicidal situation for the credibility and the future of Badminton, negotiations are initiated between the IBF and the WBF. Despite these attempts at reconciliation, the conflict lasts until 26 May 1981. On this date, the IBF representative Stellan Mohlin and the WBF representative Air Marshal Dawee Chullaspya, sign a unification agreement in Tokyo. They settle most of the differences at the source of the split, reaching compromises on the topics of voting modalities, Chinese integration and national representation in decision-making.

Following the settlement of the crisis, the Chinese have a free rein with which to impose their domination. At its first participation in the Thomas

Cup event in 1982, China beats Indonesia, holder of the previous four Thomas Cups, at the Royal Albert Hall in London, 5-4. This victory is secured in the presence of Her Majesty, Queen Elizabeth, and Prince Philip.

In 1984, there are three important modifications to the World Team Championships. From now on, the Thomas and Uber Cups will take place the same year with the number of matches to be reduced from nine to five (three singles and two doubles) and the interval between successive events reduced from three to two years.

In the men's game, Indonesia gets revenge over China. As for the women, the Chinese are successful in their first participation in the Uber Cup. They beat England 5-0 in the final, thereby ending the long period of Japanese domination extending over five Uber Cups (since 1966). In 1986, China would go one better achieving the double winning both Thomas and Uber Cups.

Second appearance at the Olympic Games

Badminton makes an Olympic Games comeback in Seoul in 1988. Although it is still an exhibition sport, it is scheduled for inclusion at the Barcelona Olympics. The 90th session of the International Olympic Committee held a few years earlier in Berlin concludes that *"Badminton will be on the programme of the next Olympic Games in 1992... but with a limited number of players".*

Carrying on from its recent victories in the Thomas and Uber Cups, China (in Seoul) wins the mens' singles (Yang Yang), the women's singles (Han Aiping) and the men's doubles (Li Yongbo and Tian Bingyi). Only the Korean ladies pairing of Kim Yun-Ja and Chung Soo-Young, and mixed doubles team of Joo-Bong and Chung Myung-Hee manage to prevent a clean sweep for China.

During the 94th session of the IOC, the commission's report advocates the permanent inclusion of the Badminton event to the summer Games. The influence of the Olympic movement has a direct and positive effect on IBF. The International Federation can expand its prestige with a wave of new members : Italy, Syria, Greece, as well as Guatemala, Argentina, Madagascar, the Seychelles, Samoa and Fiji. These countries which had until now considered Badminton as a pleasant pastime are unable to resist the prospect of conquering new Olympic medals.

A new international competition : "The Sudirman Cup"

Before this supreme recognition, a new world competition is created at the instigation of the IBF. For the moment, the mixed doubles still doesn't have its own team competition equivalent to the Thomas and Uber Cups. The "Sudirman Cup", as the World Mixed Team Championships, remedies this missing link.

Indonesia hosts this new tournament in 1989. The trophy is a tribute to Dick Sudirman, vice-president of the IBF and recognised as one the founding members of Indonesian Badminton. Twenty-eight teams participate in the inaugural tournament. Playing at home, Indonesia wins the title. In 1991, a year before the Barcelona Olympics, Korea would win the cup.

The Barcelona Olympic Games are just around the corner. In order to reach its quota of 192 players at the games, the IBF modifies its system of qualification to satisfy the requirements of the IOC : each country has the opportunity of sending its best players to the Games, and each continent is represented. Mixed doubles is not included. This would have to wait another four years. A technical hitch when one remembers the first All-England Championships in 1898 had excluded the singles and included the doubles.

Barcelona '92 : official inclusion to the Olympic Games

Bearing in mind all the titles picked up over the preceding years, the Chinese, the Indonesians, and the South Koreans are clear favourites to obtain the first gold medals.

In the singles, Indonesia's Susi Susanti wins the ladies' singles two hours before her fiancé and future husband Allan Budi Kusuma emulates her achievement in the men's event. On their return to Jakarta they would receive a hero's welcome, a huge parade would be organised in their honour with a procession in an open car with a giant shuttlecock fixed on top. These are the first two gold medals won by Indonesia in the Olympic Games since their revival by the Baron de Coubertin.

In doubles, the Koreans win the men's doubles thanks to Park Joo Bong and Kim Moon Soo, and for the ladies the honours go to Hwang Hye Young and Chung So Young. The Chinese are very disappointed, after dominating the recent Thomas and Uber Cup tournaments, to come away from Barcelona without an Olympic title in Badminton. Asian domination in the discipline is therefore complete. Only Denmark's Thomas Stuer Lauridsen wins a consolation bronze medal for Europe in the singles.

Danish surprise at Atlanta '96

Atlanta hosts the 1996 Games and the Danish player Poul Erik Hoyer Larsen wins gold in the men's singles. Notwithstanding this player's undeniable talent having brought him victories in two AEC's and seven European titles, his Olympic triumph is a surprise. The Asians and particularly the Chinese have been at the summit of world Badminton for years. But China's Dong Jiong is overcome in the final by Larsen's determination.

South Korea is the most successful Asian nation in these Games. Bang Soo Hyun wins the ladies' singles, while Kim Dong Moon and Gil Young Ah beat another Korean pairing in the first ever Olympic mixed doubles final. Indonesia's Ricky Subagja and Rexy Mainaky ease to victory in the men's doubles. China's Ge Fei and Gu Jun win the ladies doubles.

This second participation of Badminton at the Olympics is a huge success especially from the point of view of the media attention it draws, with more than a billion television viewers watching the Badminton finals worldwide.

Chinese superiority in Sydney

In the Sydney Olympics 2000, 172 players from 20 different national associations participate. Indonesia leads the list with 19 players followed by China with 18 players.

The 23 year-old Dane Peter Gade Christensen, head of the world rankings, is one of the favourites for gold but is beaten in the semi-finals by China's Ji Xinpeng who wins gold defeating the Indonesian Hendrawan in the final. In the men's doubles, the Indonesians Candra Wijaya and Tony Gunawan win gold with the Koreans taking silver and bronze.

The Chinese are hot favourites in the ladies singles. Indeed, six of their players occupy the first seven world ranking positions. Ye Zhaoying and Dai Yun are their highest ranked players but it is their compatriot Gong Zhichao who wins gold. Europe takes silver with Denmark's Camilla Martin and the favourite Ye Zhaoying picking up the bronze. There is a clean sweep of the medals for China in the ladies doubles with defending champions Ge Fei and Gu Jun regaining the title they won in Atlanta. Finally, in the mixed doubles, the world's number one pair Zhang Jun and Gao Ling of China confirms its supremacy. There is good news at last for England with its first Olympic medal. Simon Archer and Joanne Goode win a well-deserved bronze medal for Badminton's founding nation.

At the dawn of the 21st century, Badminton has finally achieved Olympic status after a long struggle for recognition. Asia has dominated the big international competitions since the Second World War winning most of the Thomas and Uber Cups, Sudirman Cups and World Championships. It was therefore logical to see this continent winning most of the medals at the first three Olympics. Nevertheless, a handful of Danish and British players such as Lauridsen, Larsen, Simon Archer and Joanne Goode manage to save the face of European Badminton by getting themselves on the honour's list.

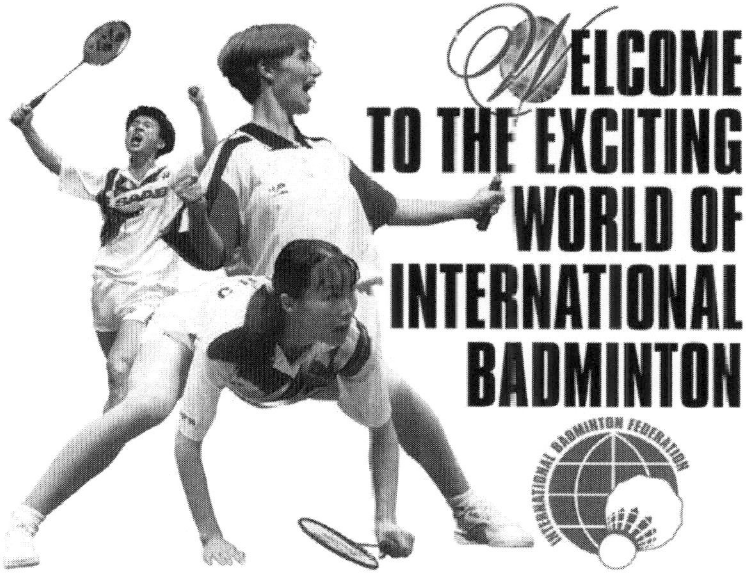

ASIAN GAMES IV
DJAKARTA 1962
150
REPUBLIK INDONESIA

第36回国民体育大会記念
36th National Athletic Meet
First Day of Issue Oct. 13, 1981

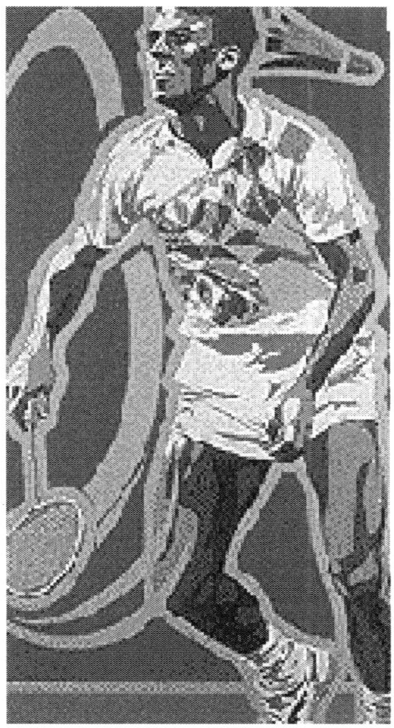

BADMINTON

Olly
Sydney 2000
badminton

5 DOLLARS
Sydney 2000

Sydney
2000
GAMES
GAMES OF THE XXVII OLYMPIAD
45c
OLYMPICS 2000 SYDNEY NSW 2000
15 SEP 2000
Badminton
FIRST DAY
OF NEW
'SYDNEY OLYMPICS 2000'
PICTORIAL POSTMARK
Paul Hoyer-Larsen (DEN)
Susi Susanti (INA)
Olympic Champions..
Badminton
15th September 2000

Kevin
Han
BADMINTON
USA
OLYMPICARD
UPPER DECK

Sydney 200

MILO
EON

Chapter 8 :
Variations of the Shuttlecock Game

Although Badminton is honoured in the 1990's by becoming an Olympic sport, this has not brought about the disappearance of the traditional game of battledore and shuttlecock. In other words, with different rules and in a variety of forms, the use of a shuttlecock is still in practice in games other than modern Badminton.

Man is constantly striving to escape from routine. That's why from a common base that is a feathered shuttlecock, he has tried to adapt it to specific cultural or geographical contexts, or else to his momentary whim.

New accessories for the shuttlecock game

In his book, *Jeux des Jeunes filles de tous les pays* (1823), X. le Prince describes a variation of the game. According to him, this new source of distraction originated in France : *"The eternally clever French have just invented a variation of the shuttlecock game : the equipment is a cornet-shaped sleeve. This game has been adopted everywhere for several years and still seems to be fashionable".*

A few years later, the historian H-R. d'Allemagne describes (in *Sports et Jeux d'adresse*) this new and fashionable game of the beginning of the 20th century : "In this leisure amusement, a leather or cardboard cornet fixed on to the end of a 30 cm stick replaces the racket. The shuttlecock is received by the cornet and returned to the opponent who receives it in a similar manner. This game is more difficult than the ordinary shuttlecock game... In 1829, the Duchess of Berry who was a talented player, counted up to 200 points without missing the cornet once".

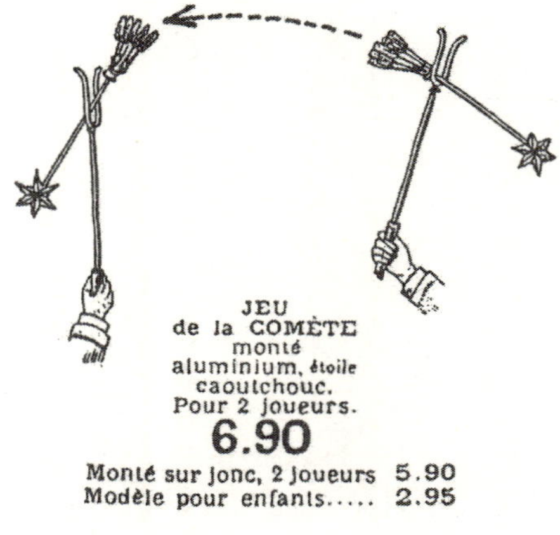

Another variation is created at this time but without really taking off. It is briefly described in a French toy manufacturer's catalogue under the name "*Jeu de la comète*" ("comet game"). The game consists of catching a stick – with a star attached to one end and a shuttlecock to the other – with a long aluminium fork.

From Table Tennis to "Table Badminton"

Following the success of the inaugural Wimbledon tournament in 1877, it is only a matter of time before the pioneers try to create a miniature form of the game in order to adapt it to people's lounges. Patents are signed in England and North America at the beginning of the 1890's under various names : "Gossima", "Parlour Table Game", "Table Lawn Tennis", "Pom Pom", and "Ping Pong".

At the turn of the century in England, table Tennis becomes a big hit in society. Tournaments are organised up and down the country. For commercial reasons, two rival Federations are created in 1901 : the Table Tennis Association and the Ping Pong Association. A specialised magazine is initiated in 1902 with the title *Table Tennis and new Pastimes* while the first teaching manual about this new game (*Ping Pong and how to play it*) comes out the same year written by the champion Arnold Palmer.

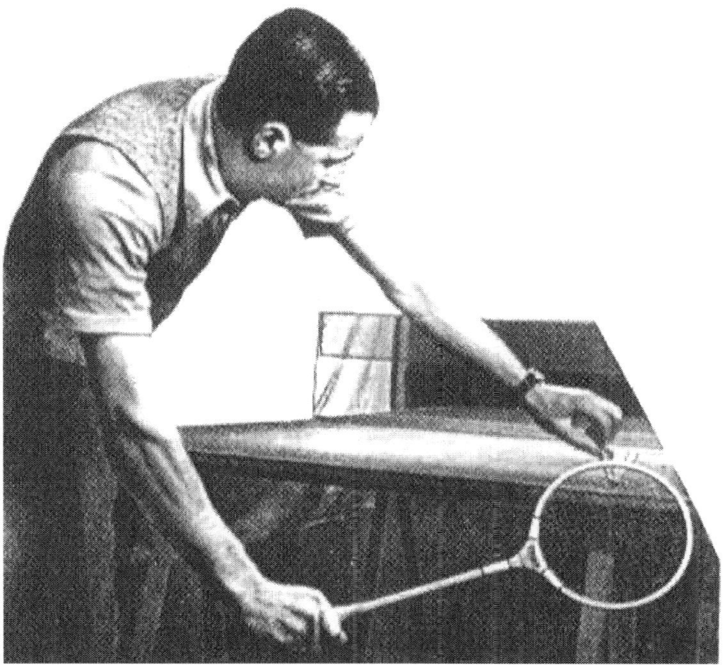

Therefore two new racket sports emerge at the end of the 19th century to partner Lawn-Tennis : Badminton and Table Tennis. Equipment makers would soon try and join them together. A short article appears on 6th March 1901 in the magazine *Lawn Tennis and Croquet* to announce the innovation launched by the firm Slazenger & Sons : *"All Badminton players will hear with pleasure that "Wiff Waff" or "Table Badminton" is to appear very shortly. That the game will prove immensely popular there is not the slightest doubt ; indeed, considering what an excellent game table Tennis is, it is surprising Badminton has not been adapted to the table before now. The price, we understand, will be about 7s 6d".*

Even if it is unlikely that this game ever really becomes popular, the equipment makers don't give up trying. Adverts praising "Arena Table Badminton" (manufactured by British Music & Tennis Strings LTD in Hackney, London), the most developed version of the game, still appear in the 1930's in *The Badminton Gazette* : *"The advertisers suggest we lead the queue to a new delight when the courts are full and waiting players are becoming discontented – not a toy but a first class, expertly-made miniature edition of a match Badminton set. All the demon speed of the real game is there in this new wonder that is setting the Sports Word afire".*

In 1935, E.E. Natali writes a book entitled *Table Badminton*. It describes the basic rules and gives advice on how to play table Badminton correctly : *"The primary objective of the game is to hit the shuttlecock over the net. Where possible, play on a table 9 feet by 5 feet at a Height of 2 foot 6 inches from the floor with the net* $13^{1/2}$ *inches above the table. The special shuttlecock has been evolved in relation to these standard measurements. The rules are few and simple. They can almost be summarised by saying that you have to hit the shuttlecock without it touching the table, hit over the net but not beyond the end or side of the table. Scoring is as in table Tennis".*

He explains the comparative lack of success of the game by the problems encountered making shuttlecocks adapted to the game's characteristics (table size, closeness of the players, lack of bounce). Lastly, this original but slightly artificial game would never really create an audience for itself.

In the 1930's, a new type of Badminton tries to break through.

The shuttlecock game played with tambourine or hoop

Except for the racket, this new game resembles the traditional shuttlecock game. A tambourine replaces a racket. The tambourine has a leather handle attached with which to hold it. At this time, the game is called "Bing-it". In the sixties, the equipment manufacturer Sportcraft brings out the game under the name *Tamburelli*. According to the suggested rules, the players can either exchange rallies until a mistake is made or else use a net as in Badminton : *"Here is a pleasant, active game, in which a shuttlecock – or sponge ball – is batted back and forth with Italian drums or tamburelli constructed of genuine skins stretched tightly over sturdy wooden frames. Young and old can enjoy this fascinating pastime. Tamburelli games may be fast or slow, depending on the age and size of the players".* Game is 21 points. A point is scored in every play including service. Players hold the tamburelli by inserting the three middle fingers into the strap and gripping the inside of the frame. It is legitimate to hit with either side to the tamburelli, and except on service, to use either underhand or overhand strokes. *Tamburelli* is undeniably inspired by other ball games played with a ball in Italy or France.

We can also find on the market a game entitled "Areola Hoop Badminton", which instead of being played with a net is played with a hoop, with the aim of hitting the shuttlecock through it. The game can be played indoors or outdoors.

"Batinton" or the military version of Badminton

Another variation of Badminton is a direct result of the shortage of materials imposed by the First World War. In 1918, a New Zealand General based in Cologne asks the officer in charge of leisure activities to find a form of physical exercise that is likely to suit all the soldiers. It is up to Lieutenant Patrick Hanna to reconcile 30,000 soldiers with confined playing space.

Baptised "Batinton", two or four players exchange rallies above the net on a rectangular court not bigger than a tenth of the size of a Tennis court. The aim is therefore to allow 40 soldiers to unwind on a reduced surface area. However the lack of shuttlecocks would soon send this activity into oblivion.

"Batinton" comes back into fashion for identical reasons at the beginning of the Second World War. This time the players are Australian. The participants use a table Tennis bat with a slightly extended handle. The game does not go completely out of fashion after the war, but would be modernised in the fifties at the same time as the appearance of plastic shuttlecocks and rackets.

Peteca : Brazil's second national sport

We have seen some versions of Badminton where a tambourine, a cornet or the Ping-Pong bat replaces the racket. Other games which in some countries have developed into full blown sports, do away with an instrument to strike the shuttlecock altogether.

In Brazil, the players use their hands to hit the shuttlecock. In the spirit of the primitive "*Jeu de paume*" and other ancestral pastimes of Southern American tribes (such as the Tupian Indians), *Peteca* is in fact a kind of Badminton played with the hand. The term "*peteca*" is of Indian origin and means "hit and shuttlecock". Traditionally, the shuttlecock's base is made of leather or corn leaves with some feathers attached.

The players strike the shuttlecock to each other with the hand trying to avoid it hitting the ground. It is in fact this form of the game that the Europeans would discover in 1920, when Brazilian athletes participating in the Anvers Olympics would kill time during the breaks between competitions by hitting some shuttlecocks.

Later, the game becomes more sophisticated with a net being erected between the participants. The court is itself strictly defined. It evolves therefore, from a simple pastime to one of Brazil's most popular sports along with Football. Today, a Federation and a set of rules give structure to more than 10,000 Peteca clubs up and down the country. The "Metropolitan Cup" attracts 4,000 participants and more than 20,000 spectators. Accessible to both licensed and non-licensed players, there are several categories of player according to age and sex with some players over 80 years old.

Peteca has subsequently crossed the oceans and been adopted by other countries, won over by the game's simplicity and physical engagement.

From Peteca to Indiaca

In 1936, a teacher of physical education, Karl Krohn, imports the game of *Peteca* into Germany. A German company – the Bremshev Sport Gmbh – deals with the manufacturing of shuttlecocks as well as the promotion of this new sport. This new sport is known under the name of *Indiaca.* This is a synthesis of the term "Indian" – as a reference to its South American origins – and *Peteca* – similar to the Brazilian game.

The similarity with Badminton is striking as *Indiaca* shares most of the rules apart from the fact that it is played six against six on a different sized court, better suited to hitting the shuttlecock with the hand. *Indiaca* is played in several countries and even achieves a degree of popularity in Japan with almost a million enthusiasts.

In other regions of the world, especially in Asia, disciples of the shuttlecock game favour the foot over the hand. As we have already seen, the use of the foot to kick the shuttlecock is a centuries-old pastime. As a leisure activity or as a means of keeping warm in the winter, the aim of the game was to exchange rallies without the shuttlecock hitting the floor. The players would often be placed in a circle. The player who failed to hit the shuttlecock back to his partners had to leave the ring. The winner would be the last one left after everyone else has been eliminated.

Survival and current practice of "shuttlecock kicking" in Asia

Widely in practice throughout the different Asian countries, "shuttlecock-kicking" is known under a variety of names. The rules vary also from one region to another.

In the People's Republic of China, shuttlecock-kicking, which is derived from the secular *Ti-jian-zi*, is widely played by children. However, since the fifties, the traditional game has also been transformed into a real sport.

Jianqiu (literally "shuttlecock kicking ball game") is played between two teams of three single players, like Badminton, over a 1.50 m. high net. On each side is a 1 m. x 1 m. "throwing area" in the right corner near the net and a "serving area" – a semicircle within the court with its 2 m-long diameter overlapping the middle section of the baseline. The shuttlecock is composed of two feathers fixed to a base made from three layers of sheep skin and two metal coins (13-15 cm high with a weight of 8-10 grams). The shuttle is served first by a player in the throwing area who throws it to his team-mate standing within the serving area ; then it is kicked over the net to the opponents' side. Play is started by one side serving to the other, with each side thereafter allowed to hit the shuttlecock three times before it must cross the court. Before or after kicking the shuttle, a player is allowed to touch it with any part of his body above the knees except the upper limbs. The shuttle is volleyed back and forth over the net until either side commits a fault. The games are played up to 15 points. A Federation also runs this very physical sport.

In Korea, we recall that the game is called *Jeigi-chagi*. Today, it is still very popular with young boys and girls playing it in the street. The shuttlecocks that used to be made of feathers are today made out of paper and coins. In Macao, a similar game is called *Chiquia*. A stamp from the year 1999 indeed pays tribute to this national game. *Chap-teh* is still played in Malaysia and especially in Singapore. Once again, the game is particularly popular with children.

Finally, in Vietnam, *Da cau* has also come back into fashion. Originally, the shuttlecock was made of metal pieces and feathers. Today, it tends to be in plastic and rubber, which also makes it more resilient. This street sport even has its own space in Hanoi, the lake Hoan Kiem. Every morning, virtuosos of this sport display their talent for all to see, sending the shuttlecock back and forth over a net. This game is so popular among the people and it possesses such physical virtues that the Education Ministry has decided to include it in the school curriculum.

This game has a rival in the form of another traditional game played in Asia with similar rules but with a ball.

This ball game, the *Sepak raga*, was created by the Malayan royal family about five centuries ago. *Sepak* and *raga* respectively mean "hit" and "ball". Like the other games previously described, it was first performed in a circle with the players taking it turns to hit a woollen ball.

This game undergoes significant transformation in the 1930's. In 1935, for King George V's jubilee, a game of *Sepak raga* is played in the Malayan province of Negeri Sembilan on a Badminton court. This constitutes the birth of a new game, which becomes very popular in Penang. In 1945, the region's players merge together the rules of *Sepak raga* and the rules of Volleyball. The first competition is held at the Swim Club. The game would spread rapidly throughout the rest of the peninsula as well as in other South East Asian countries.

The Malayans create an Association on 25 June 1960. The following year, in Kuala Lumpur, representatives from different Asian states establish a body of common rules. The game receives recognition in 1965 when it is included in the South East Asian Games. At the same time, the Asian Federation of Sepaktakraw (fusion of the Malaysian term "*sepak*" and the Thai expression "*takraw*" which means "woollen ball") is created and the game becomes a separate discipline at the Asian Games. Thirty years later, an International Federation of Sepaktakraw would be formed in order to govern the sport on a world scale of about twenty countries (including Australia, USA, Great Britain, Germany and Egypt).

A French speciality, Pilou

In Europe, a local game bears a close resemblance to Asian shuttlecock kicking. It is *Pilou* and it comes from the south of France. It originates in the 1940's when the old 25-centime coins, which have holes in the middle, are taken out of circulation. *Pilou* is played with a piece of paper threaded through the coin's hole. During the 60's, the game is in decline and even seems to have been completely abandoned. However it experiences a revival in 1987 as the inhabitants of Nice are seeking to promote their regional identity. During the summer of 1988, just for fun they would organise the first "Pilou World Championships".

Today it has become a very popular street game amongst students. It can be played in a variety of ways : solo juggling, free passing, with Tennis net, and especially with circles painted on the ground. Either in twos or in fours, the aim is to try to drop the *Pilou* in the circle of your opponent.

As we have seen, and not without surprise given the development of modern Badminton the game of shuttlecock has remained popular. This can be explained by its local and regional connotations. Over the last 2,000 years, it has therefore been able both to develop into a codified Olympic sport, while preserving at the same time its roots, its popular interest value, and maintaining its many different ways of making the shuttlecock flutter.

ET VIVE LE
PILOU !
E VIVA LO PILO !
Sous la direction scientifique de
André GIORDAN et José MARIA

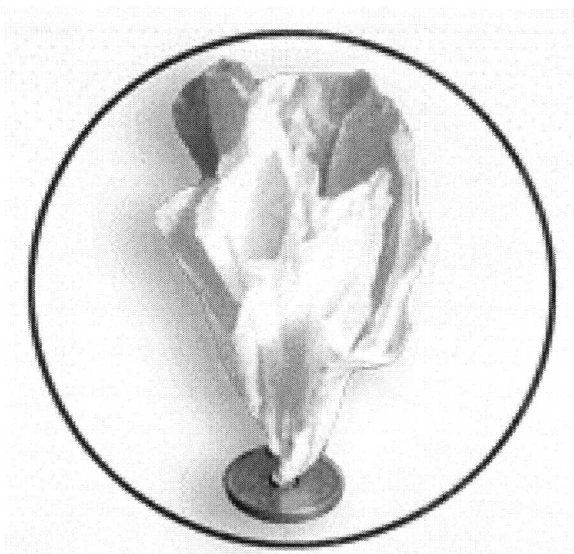

PAT HANNA

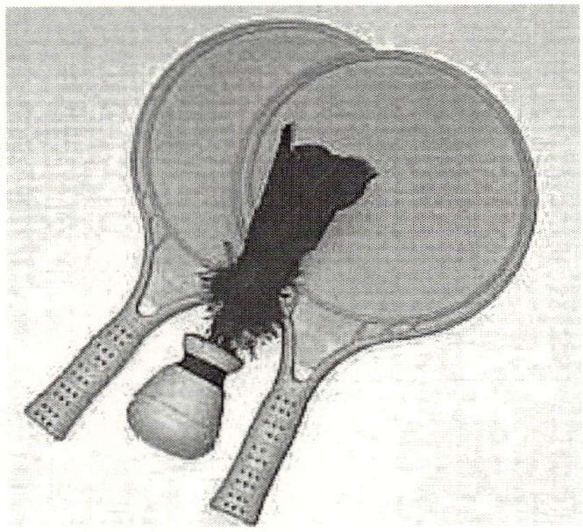

INTERNATIONAL INDIACA ASSOCIATION

IIA

Chapter 9 : Badminton, a Ball Game Played… with a Shuttlecock

In the previous chapters, we have traced Badminton's long journey from the ancient shuttlecock game to an organised, codified, universal sport attracting increasing media attention. Indeed, the universal dimension is logical given the traces of the game found in ancient civilisations all around the globe.

However, this vast panorama only goes some way to explaining the uniqueness of this sport. How does it differ from other sports ? Why take an interest in this shuttlecock sport that can be seen as little more than a child's amusement, slightly improved but nevertheless outmoded ? Finally, to which family does the game of Badminton belong ?

Badminton : a one-to-one confrontation

Badminton belongs to the category of ball games.

As the hand is arguably man's most useful tool, it is logical to observe that the ball has such an important place in "spheristic" games and more generally in recreational activities. In the case of round-shaped objects from marbles to larger balls, it is more natural to receive and send back with the hand or with an instrument that is just an extension of the body. Whether it be called *palla*, *éteuf* or *pelote*, covered in leather, string or synthetic fabric, the ball is universally employed and the inspiration behind numerous different games and sports.

As with many ball games, Badminton is a competitive sport, insofar as the game is a medium through which to satisfy the innate need to compare one's skills to those of others. Included in the nature of competition is the notion of a combat, of a match, of stretching oneself to the limits, of overcoming an opponent. The Greek word for combat is *athlos* or *agonia*, demonstrating that the player is in fact a fighter at times subject to agony.

Rivalry does not necessary mean inequality. That explains the invention of the “handicap” to re-establish equality of both sides' chances of winning through the system of handicapping the stronger side. This principle was especially employed in the earliest Badminton competitions. Today, the principle of equal chance is sustained through categorisation according to age and sex for example.

Badminton is also a game of confrontation. This notion means a battle, a struggle or a match between two sides. The term “match” is indeed derived from the English word for the match that the artillery soldier uses to set light to powder explosives.

Badminton is therefore a one-to-one game. The notion of a side is essential. Two players or two teams are in opposition and facing each other. Sides are also defined from a topographical point of view, with each player or side occupying a defined space, separated from each other by a line (here a transversal net). This line crossing the court transforms the space into two distinct camps giving meaning to the exchanges.

The invention of the net in the 17th century is therefore a defining moment both from historical and practical points of view. It replaces the line drawn on the ground, the taut string, or the string covered with ribbons. The aim is twofold : a clearer definition of the two sides ; a validation of a correct crossing of the ball or the shuttlecock from one side to the other.

A game of alternation in a closed and limited space

Badminton is therefore a game involving "alternation" in space and time. Firstly, each player plays on one side with the net preventing incursions into the opposite camp. Secondly, each player plays in turn. A point is scored each time a rally is interrupted whatever the reason : a mistake (double hit, shuttlecock in the net or out of the court) or a winner (impossibility for the opponent to return the shuttlecock).

Badminton is also a game of relative proximity insofar as the rallies take place in a limited space, unlike the sports involving the use of big pitches (Football, Lacrosse, Hockey), or even other ball games with longer pitches (*Longue paume*, Tambourine game, *Jeu du tamis*, *Ulama*).

This limited space is rectangular. As we have seen, this has not always been the case. The hourglass shape, as if two trapezes were brought together by their small bases, was the court accepted for the first official competitions in England. This original shape (also used for lawn-Tennis, the famous "*sphairistiqué*" invented by Major Walter Clopton Wingfield), was a result of specific constraints imposed by the place where Badminton was originally played : indoor halls with side doors left open to ventilate and to allow the sport to exist in hot and humid countries. Finally, a practical consideration needs to be taken into account, notably side strings or nets allowing the central net to be fixed better, also imposed the constraint of a hourglass shaped court.

The rectangular court soon returns, however, to impose itself on the game. This shape which has already been used for a long time in the *Jeu de paume* (or "Real Tennis") is more elegant than the square and easier for the eye to orientate itself regarding the court's dimensions. There is also a certain symbolism to be interpreted in the rallies exchanged within the four cardinal points.

Badminton is an enclosed sport. Not only by the defined limits imposed by the court but also by its status as an indoor sport (at least as far as competitive Badminton is concerned). This is in order to reduce as much as possible the hazards produced by effects of the wind or the unevenness of the ground, and thus to strengthen the principle of equal and fair chance. Being a sport in an enclosed space also increases the need for strong discipline. Along with the proximity aspect, the enclosed area brings to Badminton a single space favouring speed, strategy and skill.

A game of direct exchanges

Other games are characterised by alternating shots : *Pelote basque*, Squash, Racket-ball… In all these games however, the exchanges are indirect with the ball hitting one or more walls before reception by the opponent. In Badminton, like in other sports such as Tennis, Ping-Pong and Pasaka, the exchanges are direct, without passing by a physical object.

Badminton is not a game which attempts to eliminate an opponent with physical contact, as in the "prisoners' ball game" for example (one lost if touched by the ball). Heir to the great Greek *phénindé,* Badminton can be described as a "positive game" : rather than trying to eliminate the opponent, its aim is to hit the shuttlecock out of the reach of the opponent. Badminton is therefore a game of "putting beyond reach".

The racket as a fundamental accessory

To categorise Badminton it is important to examine the types of hitting and the instrument used to hit with. Badminton is a racket sport. As with the net, the use of racket comes at the end of a period of a long evolution.

As we have seen, the first "instrument" was the hand. The hand's role in ball games was so essential that the *Jeu de paume* had been named after the "*paume*" ("palm"), the internal part of the hand that is used to hit with. To-day, the shuttlecock is still hit with the hand in several North American tribes or in the *Peteca* game.

However, in order to achieve a real and direct exchange (and not just a blocked shot), the hitting surface changed. The leather strap worn up to the wrist replaced the bare palm. The glove followed this. This "protection" was either supple or doubled with a leather patch on the palm side for increased protection. The need to protect the hand would be followed by the need to extend it. The longer the instrument, the faster and the longer the rallies. The leather glove would get longer, even becoming a separate element (*gant coque, chistera*).

The real turning point would happen at the beginning of the 16th century with the use of instruments equipped with wooden handles : wooden bat, battledore in skin, racket with strings. The objective was now not only to protect the hand but also to remove it from all contact with the ball or the shuttlecock. It is less of an extension than a replacement. It also permits better hitting and more attacking play, thanks to the rigid and flat surface.

Most ball games, including Badminton, would become as a result "per-cussion" games in a single temporal moment (receiving/sending back). It would distinguish itself from the sliding shots (with long and curved glove), and from the double shot (small *chistera*) or triple shot (big *chistera*).

Badminton is therefore a game of confrontation, with a competitive goal, based on direct and alternating exchanges with a racket and occurring in an enclosed space. But its uniqueness lies in the use of a shuttlecock, a very original accessory only to be found in Badminton.

Badminton's uniqueness distinguishing it from its neighbouring sports

To emphasise its unique character even further, it is useful to compare it to four other games – *Jeu de paume*, Tennis, Volleyball and battledore and shuttlecock – the sports that resemble Badminton more than any others.

Badminton is a modern result of the medieval *Jeu de paume* ; it inherited the net from it, the use of an instrument with a handle (a racket), a rectangular court and the very important principle of direct and short exchanges between opponents. Despite these similarities, Badminton is fundamentally different. Firstly, Real Tennis uses a sphere (a skin covered ball wrapped around a centre composed of sand or compressed cotton) and not a shuttlecock. In addition, Badminton has not retained the chasing nature of Real Tennis. Finally, its points system is in units of 15 and not numerical (with straightforward point progression).

The two main characteristics distinguishing it from modern Tennis remain the use of a shuttlecock instead of a ball, and the points system. But these two features of sports involving direct exchanges share the racket, the net, the shape of the court, and the number of possible players and team combinations.

Like Badminton, Volleyball is played within a rectangular area, with an identical points system, between two sides separated by a net (erected at a distance of 2.43 m. and not 1.53 m. like Badminton). Four traits clearly differentiate the two sports. Volleyball is played with a ball. It is played with the hand. It is exclusively a team game. Finally, and most importantly, Volleyball is a game involving passes (albeit in a limited number) between team-mates whereas Badminton as we have seen is a percussive game involving direct and alternating exchanges (only one strike allowed).

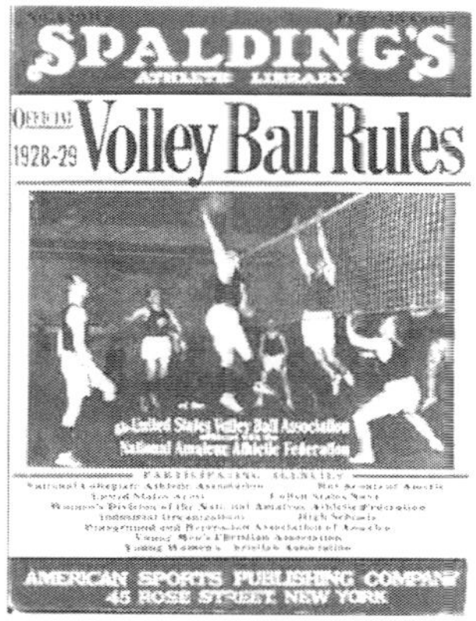

The final useful comparison in our study is to be made between Badminton and the game of battledore and shuttlecock (or *Jeu du volant*). Once again, despite sharing common elements such as the shuttlecock and the racket, these two games are very different.

"Battledore" is not a direct confrontation sport, nor it is a sport of attack and combat. It is more accurate to describe it a pastime, performing more of a leisure function than a competitive one. The aim of the game is not to force a mistake out of the opponent. On the contrary, the aim is to keep the shuttlecock in the air as long as possible. There is no winner or loser, apart from the fact that the two players try to beat the number of consecutive exchanges. This game is played in an open, unlimited space without material separation of the participants. Finally, the game has freer rules with the local players free to decide on the nature of the exchanges (long or short, free strikes or compulsory alternation between forehand and backhand…), whereas Badminton is subjected to a strict and official regulation.

Badminton's uniqueness

These observations underline the extent to which Badminton is a unique sport. Even if it shares some principles with other sports, its nature is special and symbolised by the use of a shuttlecock instead of a ball.

Even if we have seen the differences separating Badminton from battledore and shuttlecock, the former is clearly heir to the latter, and its source therefore dating back to the roots of civilisation. The blossoming of modern athletic sports in late 19th century England, has tended to cloud the true roots of Badminton, that is to say the universality of its origins, and the uniqueness of its spirit, and traditions.

With so many points in its favour, it is sure to climb one last final hurdle, that of achieving greater media popularity.

Match Point

One of the reasons why the history of Badminton is so interesting is its slow coming to maturity. It took several centuries to evolve from a simple, free and non-codified game, to a modern, professional and Olympic event.

What is equally fascinating is that following its modernisation, the latter has not resulted in the disappearance of the former. Unlike other sports, (Football replacing the *Soule*, Golf replacing "Pall-mall") Badminton and the shuttlecock have managed to coexist.

The numerous works of art representing shuttlecock matches over the globe testify to the perennial nature of the shuttlecock game. Similarly, the game of battledore and shuttlecock has remained one of the favourite sea-side leisure activities. All over the world holidaymakers can observe those games on the beach. Without knowing it, these beach players are "peloting" as did their English, French or Japanese ancestors in the 15th century.

Also, the most socially and culturally ancient versions have not disappeared. The shuttlecock game continues to be played with the hand or the foot in Asia and South America. Surprisingly, it has also helped bring about new sports combining the rules of Badminton and Volleyball.

As for Badminton, its universality, the permanency of its tournaments (Thomas, Sudirman and Uber Cups) as well as its accession to the Olympic Games has made it one of the most popular sports in the world.

Naturally, it has still to establish itself as a big media sport and to do this it would need to take inspiration from the game's popularity in Asia. Its fame also needs to be spread to regions still widely uninterested in the sport : the Middle East, Southern Europe, Latin America and Africa. Certainly, its admission into the Olympics and the possibility it provides for nations to win more medals will help it in its future development.

More than a century old already, one can only hope that its longevity will match that of the traditional game of battledore and shuttlecock.

Bibliography

Books on Badminton :

- S.M. Massey, *Badminton*, William Clowes & Sons, 1911
- G. Thomas, *The Art of Badminton*, Hutchinson, 1923
- N. Ferrers-Nicholson & S.G. Hedges, *The Art of Badminton*, Methuen & Co, 1934
- C.H. Jackson & L.A. Swan, *Better Badminton*, Barnes & Company, 1939
- B. Uber, *That Badminton Racket*, Hutchinson, 1949
- E. Choong & F. Brundle, *The Phoenix Book of Badminton*, Phoenix Sports Books, 1956
- J. Poole, *Badminton*, Goodyear Publishing Company, 1969
- M.V. Bloss & RS. Stanton, *Badminton*, Wm. C. Brown Publishers, 1971
- B. Adams, *The Badminton Story*, British broadcasting Corporation, 1980
- P. Davis, *The Encyclopaedia of Badminton*, Robert Hale, 1987

Books on other games and sports :

- F-A. de Garsault, *L'art du paumier-raquettier*, 1767
- J. Strutt, *The Sports and Pastimes of the People of England*, 1801
- X. Le Prince, *Jeux des Jeunes filles de tous les pays*, 1823
- F. Dillaye, *Les Jeux de la Jeunesse*, Hachette, 1885
- H-R. d'Allemagne, *Sports et Jeux d'adresse*, Hachette, 1889
- G. Vuillier, *Plaisirs et Jeux depuis les origines*, J. Rothschild, 1900

- J.M. Heathcote, *Tennis, Lawn Tennis, Rackets, Fives*, The Badminton Library, 1903 (new edition in 1987 by Ashford Press Publishing)
- S. Culin, "Games of North American Indians (monograph)", *Twenty-Fourth Annual Report of the Bureau of American Ethnology*, Washington, D.C., United States, 1907.
- S. Culin, *Games of the Orient*, 1958 (originally published in 1895 under the title *Korean Games, with Notes on the Corresponding Games of China and Japan*).
- G. Kutscher ("Ceremonial Badminton in the ancient culture of Moche", Proceedings of the 32nd International Congress of Americanists, 1956. Copenhagen, 1958.
- G. Gurney, *Tennis, Squash and Badminton Bygones*, Shire Publications LTD, 1984
- J-M. Mehl, *Jeux au Royaume de France du 13e au 16e siècle*, Fayard, 1990
- G. Bonhomme, *De la paume au Tennis*, Découvertes Gallimard, 1991
- H. Gillmeister, *Tennis, a Cultural History*, Leicester University Press, 1997
- J. Rice, *Start of Play*, Prion Books Limited, 1998
- A. Giordan & J. Maria, *Et vive le Pilou !,* Z'éditions, 1998
- J. Arramendy, *Le Jeu, la balle et nous*, Atlantica, 2000.

Notes on the Illustrations

Cover page :

1. Colour card entitled “Maiko girl playing Hanetsuki”, Japan.
2. Baxter & Bros. coloured chromolithography of three children playing with a shuttlecock.
3. Colour photo of Xia Xuanze, China.

Chapter 1 :

4. Victorian colour engraving by Thomas Allom (1804-1872), “Playing at shuttlecock with feet”, c. 1843.
5. Black and white engraving “Shuttlecock in China”, *Journal de la Jeunesse*, France, c.1875.
6. Watercolour on silk by Le Chuon, Vietnam : “Kick a shuttle-cock”.
7. Drawing of a Miao shuttlecock.
8. Printing “Korean shuttlecock-kicking” in S. Culin (*Games of the Orient*, 1958)
9. Black and white printing of a “shuttlecock play” (*Hago Asobu*), Japan, in S. Culin.
10. Colour photo of modern *hagoita.*
11. Drawing of a Zuñi shuttlecock.
12. Drawing of a wooden bat by the Bellacoola tribe, British Columbia, in S. Culin (“Games of the North American Indians”, *24th annual Report of the Bureau of Ethnology*, 1902-03).
13. Drawing of bat and shuttlecock by the Makah tribe, Washington, in S. Culin.
14. Drawings of shuttlecocks used by the Zuñi Indian tribe, New Mexico, in S. Culin.
15. Reproduction of a Moche vase painting (North Peru), in G. Kutscher (“Ceremonial Badminton in the ancient culture of Moche”, International Congress of Americanists, 1956)

Chapter 2 :

37. Watercolour by Diane Sperling (1791-1862), representing her brother "playing for the shuttlecock" with Mrs Van Hagen, c. 1812. England.

Chapter 3 :

38. Photo of the game of Badminton played in India. 1867. Unknown origin. From *The Badminton Story*, B. Adams.
39. The game of Badminton in an Indian setting. Drawing in *The Field* magazine. 1874-75.
40. Hourglass Badminton court. *The Field*, 18/10/1873. Title : "Badminton rules, Simla, as adopted at Muree".
41. Photo of a game of Badminton at Monzong Road, India. c. 1912. Unknown origin.
42. Colour painting of the Badminton House (England), mid-18th century.
43. Front page of a book by Cavendish : *The Games of Lawn-Tennis and Badminton*, 1876.
44. Black and white drawing in the *Humoristiche Blatter* journal. Vienna. By F.G. Author's collection.
45. Colour printing entitled "The new game of Badminton in India" by M.E.E., in *The Graphic*, 25/04/1874. Author's collection.
46. Coloured drawing in *Punch, or the London charivari*, 8/07/1876. Author's coll.
47. Baxter & Bros. coloured chromolithography of three children playing with a shuttlecock. Author's collection.
48. Coloured chromolithography of a little girl with shuttlecock and battledore. France. Author's collection.
49. "Damen Moden 1860". Publicity card for Liebig. Author's collection.
50. Coloured illustration in *Les Jeux des Jeunes garçons*. Nepveu Publisher, Paris, c. 1830.
51. Coloured chromolithography of young child with a huge shuttlecock. Author's collection.
52. Rackets, shuttlecocks, box and card. Private collection.
53. Photo of a game of Badminton, *Harper's*. 1891.

Chapter 4 :

Chapter 5 :

Chapter 6 :

Chapter 7 :

114. Photo of Zhang Jun & Gao Ling (China). Mixed doubles gold medal in Sydney.

Chapter 8 :

115. Illustration of the "Jeu du cornet". From a toy manufacturer's catalogue. France.
116. Illustration of the "Jeu de la comète" (comet game). 19th century. France. Author's collection.
117. Photo of a table Badminton player. From an Arena Table Badminton set. England.
118. Photo of the official Tamburelli rules. Sportcraft Sports Games.
119. Photo of the Areola Hoop Badminton set.
120. Front page of a Brazilian book on "Peteca" : *Peteca : esporte ou recreaçao ?*
121. Photo of a red Indiaca shuttlecock.
122. Stamp from Korea representing "jeigi-chagi", 1996.
123. Stamp from the Republic of China representing the traditional "ti-jian-zi".
124. Photo of a pilou shuttlecock. France.
125. Front page of *Et vive le Pilou*, by A. Giordan and J. Maria, France, 1998.
126. Black & White photo of a "Pilou" game.
127. Pilou shuttlecock.
128. Photo of Patrick Hanna (1888-1973), founder of the "batinton" game.
129. Set of "Tennis-Indiaca".
130. Colour drawing of "Peteca" player.
131. Logo of the International Indiaca Association.
132. Photo of an Indiaca player.
133. Modern poster of "Jeagi". Korea. Unknown origin.
134. Photo of a "da cau" player. Vietnam. Unknown origin.
135. Photo representing children playing at shuttlecock with the foot. Korea.

Chapter 9 :

136. Photo of a friendly match of Badminton. Unknown origin.
137. Coloured engraving of the "*Jeu de paume*", played rue Scribe, Paris. 18th century.
138. The Wingfield's lawn Tennis court (hour-glass shape), from *The Major's game of Lawn Tennis*, by Wingfield, The Raquet & Tennis Club, NY, USA.
139. Painting of a young Italian Tennis player. Italy, 1570.
140. Coloured engraving by Crispin de Pass, 1608. France.
141. Colour photo of the Hampton Court, wooden Real Tennis court built by Henry VIII prior to 1532 (The present court was constructed for Charles I in 1625). England.
142. Colour painting of Frederic Henry, Prince of Orange, playing Tennis, by Adriaan van de Venne. 1626.
143. Volley Ball rules, by Spalding's Athlete Library. 1929. Author's collection.
144. Colour photo on a toy model storybook on "shuttlecock". Unknown origin.
145. Black and white humoristic Badminton. Unknown origin.